FANCHISE
YOUR FRANCHISE

ALSO BY these authors

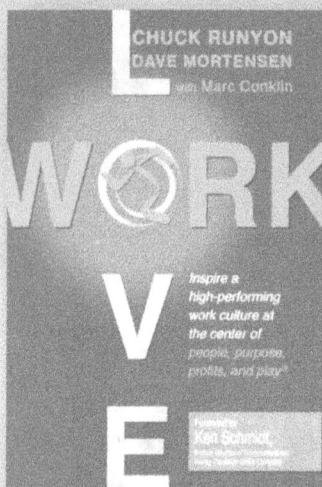

LOVE WORK

Inspire a high-performing work culture at the center of people, purpose, profits and play®

By **Chuck Runyon & Dave Mortensen**
with Marc Conklin

Foreword by Ken Schmidt, Former Director of Communications, Harley-Davidson Motor Company

WORKING OUT SUCKS!

(And Why It Doesn't Have To)
The Only 21-Day Kick-Start Plan for Total Health and Fitness You'll Ever Need

By **Chuck Runyon,**
Brian Zehetner,
and Rebecca Derossett

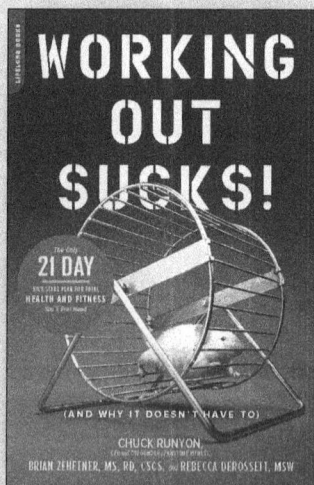

FANCHISE
YOUR FRANCHISE

CHUCK RUNYON &
DAVE MORTENSEN

Co-Founders ANYTIME FITNESS

with a foreword by *SHARK TANK'S* ROBERT HERJAVEC

GBL
PUBLISHING

GBL
PUBLISHING

For information about special discounts for bulk purchases or author interviews, appearances, and speaking engagements, please contact:

Fanchise@PurposeBrands.com

ISBN eBook   979-8-9930410-2-5
ISBN paperback   979-8-9930410-1-8

As told to, and development, certain images and editing by, Marc Conklin
Copy edited and proofread by Anne Kelley Conklin
Cover design, book layout and production by Rodney Miles

To all the franchisees, employees and purpose-driven leaders who we've shared our Fanchise *journey with over the last 20+ years.*

We're your biggest fans!

CONTENTS

FOREWORD

BY ROBERT HERJAVEC

I USED TO lie to myself that I was already as fit as I could be —
that because of time, genes, you name the excuse, reaching the next
level was impossible.

That changed a year and a half ago.

I had sold my company, so I already had more time on my hands.
Then one day, someone looked at my 7-year-old twins at the
playground and said, "Your *grandkids* are so beautiful!" It was a huge
blow — not to my ego, but to my inner dad. *How would my kids feel*

about their father looking or acting 'old'? I thought. *And how much fitter can I get so I can be with them as long as possible?*

A friend has a saying that now hangs on my wall: "We don't get old because we age. We get old because we stop training." My own mantra has always been that if you want to get somewhere you've never been, go with people who've been there. So I did that with my health. Two months after hiring a coach, surrounding myself with other people on fitness journeys, changing my diet, committing to cardio and weights, and improving my sleep, I went from 22% body fat to 13%, lost 14 pounds and gained considerable strength. I've always been a high-energy, quick-thinking guy. But mentally and physically, I've now gone from "Regular Robert" to "Robert on Steroids and Fast-Forward." I've never felt better.

Fanchise Your Franchise applies this same transformational power to franchising. Like reaching an elite fitness level, evolving from a franchise into a *Fanchise* starts with finding people who've been there. That's Chuck Runyon and Dave Mortensen — who, fittingly, have built Anytime Fitness into the world's largest fitness franchise. You couldn't ask for better coaches.

Why is franchising the best space to talk about business transformations? Over the years, I've noticed that while *Shark Tank* has empowered millions of people to believe that they can change their lives through entrepreneurship, too many of them think the number-one reason why businesses fail is "lack of capital." Don't get me wrong — money can make a good business better. But a failing business with more capital is just a business going into the ground faster.

Businesses fail because *thinking* about one is easy. Actually *running* one is hard.

That's why franchising is one of the best paths to business success. I always say to young entrepreneurs, "Why try to build everything on your own when you can invest in a proven system?" Where else can you enter the business world with branding, operations, technology and other huge challenges already solved for you?

Franchising frees you to perform at the highest level in a field that you love, but success still doesn't come easy. And that's what this book is about.

From both a franchisor and franchisee perspective, building a *Fanchise* is about taking yourself and your business to their highest levels. Chuck and Dave have accomplished that in one of the business world's most notoriously cutthroat spaces. When I asked a friend who owns a billion-dollar food company (and was a Dragon on *Dragons' Den*, the Canadian *Shark Tank*) why we got so many food product pitches, he said, "Everyone eats, so everyone thinks they know the business." Similarly, anyone who has ever jogged or lifted a weight thinks they know how to succeed in the fitness space. They have no idea how competitive it actually is.

That's why Anytime Fitness is such an incredible brand and why I have so much respect for what Chuck and Dave have accomplished. To simply survive in their industry is impressive. To scale in 20 years from one club in Minnesota to millions of members on all seven continents is unprecedented.

When you look at the entire Anytime Fitness system, it's about excellence, passion and giving people at all income levels a way to get fit like I did. Does each unit have great equipment? Yes, but so do many other gyms. More importantly, the entire Anytime Fitness franchise system has the right people, a spirit of coaching and community, and a culture of caring. You won't find a negative element of exclusivity at any level. It's pure energy.

Whether you're talking about a member or a franchisee, people join Anytime Fitness for its convenience and approachability. They stay for the culture, passion, empowerment and community. And as you'll see in the book, many of them tattoo the logo on their body because their experience changes — and in many cases *saves* — their lives.

That's a *Fanchise*.

As Chuck and Dave say in the book, they didn't just scale a product or service; they franchised a positive, accountable and contagious *culture*. That's something everyone can learn from: A successful franchise is impressive. A *Fanchise* is unstoppable.

As I've recently learned, the beauty of being human is that we don't know what we're capable of until we stretch our boundaries and *go there*. A year ago, I would have felt overjoyed to do three pull-ups. Today, I do 18 just to warm up. In the same spirit, you won't know how great your franchise and your life can be until you read this book and open your eyes to the magic of *Fanchising*.

Chuck and Dave have done the entire business world a huge favor by sharing their stories and insights in these pages. Once you see how they've pushed their own limits and changed how the franchise world thinks, you'll be inspired to do the same yourself.

And that starts *now*.

ROBERT HERJAVEC

Emmy Award Winner, Entrepreneur, Investor,
Cybersecurity Expert, Lead Shark on *Shark Tank*

September 2025

INTRODUCTION

by Chuck Runyon

> **People in the good-to-great companies became somewhat extreme in the fulfillment of their responsibilities, bordering in some cases on fanaticism.**
>
> — Jim Collins, *Good to Great*

I WALKED INTO an Anytime Fitness international conference in Tokyo in May 2024 when our master franchisee in Japan rushed up to me. "I have someone for you to meet," he said. "This is Yoshiyuki Kohata of KOHATA Holdings. He's your largest franchisee and biggest fan in the world." I thought I already knew the passion around the brand that Dave Mortensen and I co-founded in 2002. But I didn't know the half of it.

1

Dave and I love attending international Anytime Fitness conferences. We feel like we've created one of the best conferences in the U.S., and seeing a version of your lovefest translated into other languages and culture is absolutely life-changing.

But what I saw in Yoshiyuki made my jaw drop.

The first thing I noticed was that he was wearing the swag backpack from our 2016 Lake Placid conference, complete with dozens of pins from that event. Then I saw that he was wearing special shoes from our 2014 conference in Scottsdale, Arizona. His jacket was from yet another conference. Speaking through a translator, I learned that Yoshiyuki has been to 10 of our U.S. conferences.

Chuck and Yoshiyuki meet for the first time in May 2024.

Most impressive of all, I discovered that he's the single largest owner of Anytime Fitness clubs in the world. He bought his first club on September 4, 2013. He now owns 68 gyms all by himself. No partner. No private-equity money. They're all his, and he's still growing.

Yoshiyuki and I came from different worlds 6,000 miles apart. We couldn't understand a word the other said, but we didn't need a translator. I could see how happy he was, so filled with joy and pride, which made me feel the same way.

Twenty-two years after Dave, a third partner and I opened the first Anytime Fitness club in a small Minnesota town, I realized that I was standing in a country I never thought I'd see, smiling back at a man I never thought I'd know. I wasn't sharing this moment with a "franchisee." I was with a *fan* — not of me, but of a brand, an idea and a mission that has spread to every continent on the globe, and has come to mean so much more than the sum of its parts.

> **"**
>
> **Yoshiyuki and I came from different worlds 6,000 miles apart. We couldn't understand a word the other said, but we didn't need a translator. "**

How did I get to that moment, and why are Dave and I writing this book now?

First of all, we're semi-retired, so we have more time on our hands, and there's only so much golf to be played …

Second, we got here by creating something more than a franchise — something we call a *Fanchise*. We decided to write this book because more franchise businesses are starting up today than ever before, backed by more private-equity money than ever before, at a time when people need community and connection more than ever before.

We want to share what we've learned because franchise businesses have a unique opportunity to change people's lives and make a dent in the universe at the most critical time in human history. Does that sound like hyperbole? It's not. In a time of division, loss of faith in institutions and insecurities about how human beings can continue to find fulfilling work, franchise businesses are the best vehicles on the planet to deliver the meaning, purpose and economic gain we all need.

Dave and I have lived the *Fanchise* transformation. After 23 years building one of the most successful international franchise systems in history, we're ready and eager to tell our story, share our secrets and help other people do what we've done.

> **More franchise businesses are starting up today than ever before, backed by more private-equity money than ever before, at a time when people need community and connection more than ever before.**

A typical Fanchise *moment at one of our conferences, where employees, franchisees, suppliers and other partners show their fandom.*

Whether you're a franchisee or franchisor, it's no secret that a million things go into operating a successful business. Maybe you've already read or listened to all the books out there on the nuts and bolts: mastering your operations, tapping into new technologies, improving your marketing ...

This isn't one of those books. Frankly, we're assuming you already know those things. As *Good to Great* author Jim Collins might say, the insights in those other books might make you good. Maybe even *very* good. But this book is about making you *great*. And to do that, you can't just run a franchise. You have to build a *Fanchise*.

If you have serious problems at a product, service or operational level, know that you can't build a *Fanchise* on passion alone. You have to start with a solid foundation before you start climbing. Today, a proven product and tight operations are just table stakes. They'll only get you halfway up the mountain of true success, and you want to get to the peak. Because once you get there — once you create a *Fanchise* — you'll never want to come back down.

Before we climb too high, let's answer a fundamental question:

What the heck is a **Fanchise** *anyway?*

To answer that, we have to go back to the beginning. Like many franchise businesses, Anytime Fitness entered the market with a unique business model: the club that was open 24/7, featuring only the most popular weight machines and cardio equipment, where each member got a key to the club.

That was a revolutionary idea back in 2002, but you can see how easy it was to copy. As we wrote in our last book, *Love Work*:

> **All you had to do was rent 5,000 square feet in a local strip mall, load it with fitness equipment, provide 24-hour access and sell memberships.**

And that's exactly what our competitors did. Within a few years, a dozen copycat clubs were breathing down our necks. So why do most of those brands no longer exist, while we now have over 5,600 Anytime Fitness clubs all over the world, with 5 million members, and over 7,000 units in over 50 countries across the entire franchise lineup in our parent company, Purpose Brands?[1]

You could say that Anytime Fitness was the proverbial "first mover." That's true in the U.S. But we weren't the first mover when we expanded into other countries, and that's where most of our recent growth has happened.

You could point to the fact that we welcomed a private-equity partner, Roark Capital, in 2014. But one of our competitors inked a private-equity deal before we did, and they haven't matched our success, so that's not it either.

You could say it's the powerful corporate culture we dissected in *Love Work*,[2] but passion for our brand extends beyond the corporate

---

[1] Self Esteem Brands became Purpose Brands after merging with Orangetheory Fitness in November 2024. It includes Anytime Fitness, Orangetheory Fitness, Waxing the City, The Bar Method, Basecamp Fitness and Stronger U Nutrition.

[2] *Love Work* is about how centering your workplace culture on the 4 Ps of People, Purpose, Profits and Play inspires your teams to genuinely love their work, which unlocks high performance and meaningful growth.

office — into each franchise unit, into each partner and investor, and into the hearts and minds of each customer and member.

A *Fanchise* is a franchise business that, as Anytime Fitness's Global President Stacy Anderson says, "manages to franchise not only a business but also a culture, and that's a lot harder to do."

Transforming a franchise into a *Fanchise* means hitting on every cylinder and making every stakeholder feel a powerful connection to your brand. This book is for franchisees, franchisors, suppliers, private-equity investors and anyone else who makes the franchise world tick.

> **A *Fanchise* is a franchise business that, as Anytime Fitness's Global President Stacy Anderson says, 'manages to franchise not only a business but also a culture, and that's a lot harder to do.'**

The "from —> to" of a *Fanchise* transformation looks like the chart on the next page, and we want you to start making these evolutions immediately after you turn the last page of this book.

FRANCHISE		*FANCHISE*
People like your brand.	→	**People love your brand.**
Customers might wear your logo on a T-shirt.	→	**Stakeholders will tattoo your logo on their bodies.**
You feel like the business has improved your life.	→	**You feel like the business has transformed your life and the lives of those around you.**
Private-equity companies see you as a promising investment.	→	**Private-equity companies trip over themselves to invest in you.**

Along the way, we're going to take a "show, don't tell" approach — offering our insights, but also sharing photos, stories and real communications from our incredible journey.

Ready?

The lights are dimming …
The band is taking the stage …
And here comes the first chord …

WHY *FANCHISE?*

YOU'RE ABOUT TO read a lot of advice, guidance and anecdotes about what it means to go from a franchise to a *Fanchise*. It's not going to sound fast or easy. In fact, you might think to yourself, "Why bother? Is it really worth it?"

Yes, and we've distilled the "why" down to this:

Becoming a *Fanchise* will make your business more successful, resilient, valuable and fun.

If you're a bottom-line kind of person, ask yourself a question: *Are the brands that I'm a passionate fan of more or less successful than their competitors?*

Apple isn't one of the world's most successful companies because of its circuit boards. And Anytime Fitness isn't one of the world's most successful health franchises because of our treadmills. As we'll talk about in Chapter 1, fandom translates into better talent, greater loyalty and higher revenues. It also raises "lifetime value," and guess what private-equity and other investors look for?

Less understood (and grossly underrated) is the fact that a *Fanchise* has more day-to-day resilience. For the most dramatic example, see Chapter 11: "Stress-Testing Your *Fanchise*: Lessons from a Crisis." From the beginning of Anytime Fitness, we coached our franchisees to go beyond winning "members" to winning "fans" instead. One reason for that: A fan will allow you to make mistakes. A "member" or "consumer" will leave.

Is *Fanchising* hard? Of course it is, and it should be! Nothing truly valuable comes easy. We come from the fitness world, and no personal trainer is going to tell you that getting in the best shape of your life is a cakewalk. But as Anytime Fitness member-fans will tell you, it's a lot more fulfilling than sitting on a couch all day.

ANYTIME FITNESS
FANCHISE BONA FIDES

IT'S ONE THING to sign on the dotted line and start the journey of franchise ownership. It's another to permanently ink a symbol of that experience onto your own skin. Yet today, over 4,000 people around the world proudly sport tattoos of the Anytime Fitness Runningman icon — not just our employees, but our members, our franchisees and even our suppliers.

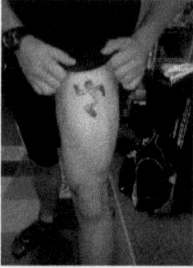

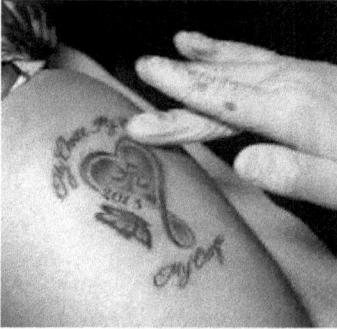

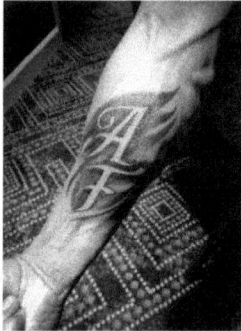
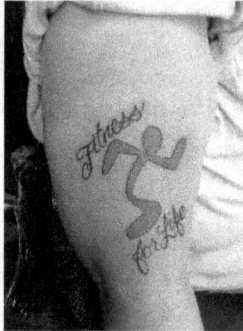
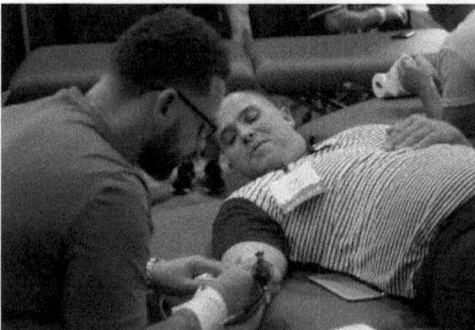

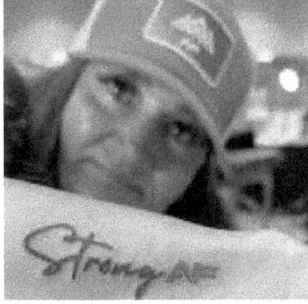

- 5,600+ Anytime Fitness clubs in 42 countries across every continent

- Over 5 million members

- 4,000+ tattoos inked on the skin of employees, members and franchisees

- Named to the *Entrepreneur* Franchise 500 for 19 years running

- AF logo flags and banners on multiple mountaintops

- 1,000+ millionaires created

- 50,000 gallons of tears shed watching Member Success Stories[3]

---

[3] An approximate number.

Anytime Fitness superheroes Captain Runningman and Xpressa visit Machu Picchu.

One of many Anytime Fitness banner displays on global mountaintops.

Scenes from Anna and Michael Dey's wedding on top of Mt. Kilimanjaro, 2014.

14

KEY MOMENTS IN ANYTIME FITNESS *FANCHISING*

2024 — Self Esteem Brands merges with Orangetheory to become Purpose Brands.

2022 — Anytime Fitness passes the 4 million-member mark.

2019 — Anytime Fitness opens on its 7th continent on the Antarctic cruise ship Magellan Explorer.

2015 — Anytime Fitness is ranked #1 Overall Franchise on *Entrepreneur* Franchise 500.

2014-15 — Anytime Fitness ranked Top Global Fitness Franchise two years in a row.

2014 — Roark Capital makes minority investment in Anytime Fitness.

2012-13 — Anytime Fitness/Self Esteem Brands voted Best Place to Work in Minnesota.

2005 — First Anytime Fitness conference (St. Paul, MN); first international club opens in Halifax, Nova Scotia; first Anytime Fitness tattoo inked; first success story shared.

2002 — First Anytime Fitness club opens in Cambridge, MN.

OUR EXPERT
FANCHISE PANEL

TO HELP US with this book, we enlisted thoughts and insights from a supergroup within the franchising world — most of whom happen to live right in our own backyard. You'll see them quoted and mentioned throughout these pages, and as part of our interview process, we asked them to tell us something about their own fandom. (We weigh in at the end as well.)

Stacy Anderson
Anytime Fitness Global President

My Fandom
"The Green Bay Packers. I grew up 15 houses away from Lambeau Field, and my parents still live there. I'm a Cheesehead through and through."

Joe Fittante
President, Larkin Hoffman[4]

My Fandom
"I love Ray Charles, and the fact that I never saw him perform is one of my big musical regrets. Legends come around only every so often, so see them when you have the chance. I once took my kids to Justin Bieber, and when my oldest cried when he came out, I thought, 'This is what it must have been like to see The Beatles in the '60s ... '"

Ron Gardner
Founding Partner, Dady & Gardner, P.A.[5]

My fandom
"I love The Eagles. *Hotel California* was the first album I ever bought, and I was 13. The harmonies are hard to beat. They created the country-rock genre. And I love what they stand for beyond their music."

---

[4] Larkin Hoffman is widely recognized as one of the nation's top law firms in franchising, representing multi-industry franchisor clients including Anytime Fitness, Burger King, Coldwell Banker, Great Clips, Radisson and Tim Hortons.

[5] Dady & Gardner, P.A., is a national leader in franchise law since 1994 and specializes in representing the legal interests of franchisees.

Jim Goniea
General Counsel, Purpose Brands, LLC

My Fandom
The Beatles. "They're just the best, though I also love The Eagles — both the band and the NFL team."

Scott Greenberg
Business Keynote Speaker & Author of *Stop the Shift Show* and *The Wealthy Franchisee*

My Fandom
"I've seen Weezer more than any other band in the last 10 years. I live in L.A., so I'm also a huge UCLA basketball fan."

Matt Haller
President & CEO
International Franchise Association

My Fandom
"You've gotta love The Rolling Stones. At this point, it's almost less about the music and more about the longevity."

Libby Junker
Senior Director of Global Implementation, Anytime Fitness

My Fandom
"I love watching the USA Ryder and Solheim Cup teams. It's great to see competitors who've been chasing each other all season come together as a team."

Chuck Modell
Franchise Attorney, Mediator and Expert Witness, Larkin Hoffman

My Fandom
"One of my daughter's boyfriends once asked her who the Florida Gators were playing that day. After she answered, he said, 'Wait, there's no school called Half-Ass U.' Our kids have only heard Florida State referred to by that name."

Brian Schnell
Partner and Chair of Franchise Practice, Faegre Drinker[6]

My Fandom
"My family will tell you that I can't make it through a Luke Bryan concert without yelling 'Luuuke!'"

---

[6] Faegre Drinker is a national law firm that specializes in helping franchisors launch, grow, protect and evolve their franchise systems.

Chuck Runyon
Anytime Fitness Co-Founder

My Fandom
"I'll always be a U2 fan. Name another band that's been that good for that long and kept all of its founding members. They've always understood that they're a team."

Dave Mortensen
Anytime Fitness Co-Founder

My Fandom
"As an old choirboy, I love good harmony and R&B, so I'm a huge Boyz II Men fan. I've also loved the Minnesota Vikings since I was a kid, so I've felt every lost opportunity since the Fran Tarkenton days."

PART I:

FANDOM
+ FRANCHISING

= *FANCHISING*

[1]

WE'RE ALL FANS OF SOMETHING

❝

Ambulance workers last night treated 125 casualties — mostly teenage girls — during the Beatles' opening concert for their British tour in the Odeon Cinema, Glasgow. [T]he foyer at times resembled a battleground. An official of St. Andrews Ambulance Association said 37 of those treated were fainting cases and 88 were suffering from hysteria. One ambulance worker complained, "Give me a Ranger-Celtic [soccer] game any day. This is just too much. **❞**

— *Glasgow Herald*, 1965[7]

---

[7] http://www.meetthebeatlesforreal.com/2015/12/beatles-fans-sent-to-hospital.html

From Chuck:

THE GREATEST JOY of my life has been raising four wonderful kids who have grown up to be high achievers filled with kindness, intellect, empathy and social skills.

Conik was born with a steering wheel in his hands, and he's convinced he could have been the next F1 champion had he not been born to a father who thinks adding windshield-washer fluid to his car is a major mechanical achievement. Delaney and Ella are the sporty middle daughters, and I enjoyed 15 years cheering, coaching and consoling them while riding the emotional roller coasters of their wins and losses in basketball, soccer and track. And after Charlie, the youngest, discovered a passion for wake surfing in the Land of 10,000 Lakes, I've been his willing accomplice driving the boat.

For those of you who haven't tried wake surfing, it requires three ingredients: a lake, a boat with ballasts and wave-making plates, and *music*. Luckily for Charlie and me, we share a music fandom. He likes the bands I grew up listening to in the '80s, '90s and 2000s, and I enjoy his playlists filled with more recent artists. As we do our wake-surfing routine under a peek-a-boo sun on a cloudy day at our cabin, we'll fill our lungs with clean northern air while mixing songs from Queen, Metallica, Bruno Mars, Elton John, Drake, Red Hot Chili Peppers, Guns N' Roses, AC/DC, Pink Floyd and Coldplay.

As our love of music grew, Charlie and I started going to concerts together. My second-, third- and fourth-favorite concert experiences of all time (Coldplay, Red Hot Chili Peppers and Metallica, respectively) were all at Soldier Field in Chicago. Windy City summers have a sweet melody all their own, and nothing beats scootering to restaurants, rating the best burgers and wheel surfing on the Lake Michigan shoreline.

But the concert that rises to the top of my list wasn't in Chicago. It also wasn't the best musical performance I've ever seen. In fact, it wasn't even the best performance I've seen by this particular band. But it was the best overall *experience.*

Some context: I graduated from high school in 1987, the same year a certain Dublin foursome released *The Joshua Tree.* This record is widely regarded as one of the best albums of all time, and it includes one of my top 10 favorite songs, "Where the Streets Have No Name." I've surfed to Bono, The Edge, Larry Mullen Jr. and Adam Clayton for nearly four decades, so when the Sphere in Las Vegas announced that U2 was going to kick off its grand opening, I knew that Charlie and I had to go.

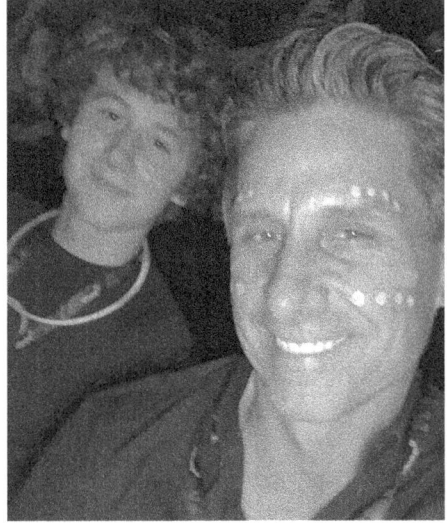

Chuck and his son Charlie get glammed out for U2 at The Sphere in Las Vegas, 2024.

We flew to Vegas, and my daughter Ella flew in from her college in San Diego. Days before, an Anytime Fitness employee and fellow U2 lover told me a key piece of intel: Opening night was going to have a neon "glow in the dark" theme. So after dinner, Ella carefully applied glow-in-the-dark paint to our faces and gave us neon glow rings to wear around our arms, necks and ankles.

An hour later, Charlie and I made the long walk through casinos and retail areas to the Sphere. (Not all musical tastes are handed down in the genes, so Ella went back to the hotel.) Oddly, we didn't see anyone else in neon. But hey, we weren't at the venue yet, right? Surely we would find our tribe as we got closer. We moved through security, still no neon. We took our seats and looked around … no one wearing face paint or body rings. To this day, I still don't know if that employee was misinformed or punking us, but we were all alone.

Maybe since most of the audience is my age, they don't want to look foolish, I thought. Anyone who knows me knows that I have no problem making an ass of myself, so I didn't care. But what I remember most is that Charlie — at the normally self-conscious age of 16 — wasn't embarrassed at all. He didn't take anything off. In fact, he did the opposite. He owned the look all night, strutting through the Vegas streets and walkways hours after The Edge strummed the evening's final chords on his Gibson Explorer.

After the concert, an *Irish Times* reporter approached us for our review, probably because we were the only two people glowing neon. The next morning, a friend in Ireland texted me after seeing a quote in the *Irish Times* about U2's opening-night performance from a young, glammed-out fan named "Charlie Runyon."

U2 was good (not great) that night, but it didn't matter. Take the Sphere's immersive audiovisual experience, add the vision of my neon son rocking out to *Joshua Tree* songs and answering questions from an Irish reporter, and it was by far my favorite concert experience.

> *I want to run; I want to hide.*
> *I want to tear down the walls that hold me inside.*
> *I wanna reach out and touch the flame*
> *Where the streets have no name.*

WHAT IS FANDOM?

We share this story about fandom because we're all "fans" of something. Lots of things, actually. But what exactly is fandom? What's the difference between liking something, appreciating it and being absolutely *fanatical* about it?

Music is a good place to start. If you're older, you might remember Beatlemania in the early 1960s. Moving forward a generation, think about the Deadheads — people who were not only fans of a band's music, but followed them as they performed all over the world and created an entire lifestyle around them. Moving closer to home, we think about the tragic death of Prince on April 21, 2016, which caused thousands of fans to gather outside the First Avenue nightclub for a spontaneous all-night party. Today, Swifties dress like their hero as they hang on her every word, analyze every lyric and sing every song at her concerts.

If music isn't your thing, then sports probably are. Four decades after Bear Bryant coached his last football game at the University of Alabama, Crimson Tide fans *still* name their babies after him. The NFL gives us the Cleveland Browns' Dawg Pound, Green Bay Packers fans dressed in foam cheeseheads and Vikings fans doing the Skol Chant. The *other* "football" gives us the Peruvian soccer fans who traveled 8,000 miles to see their men's national team play in the 2018 World Cup in Russia.[8] Then add Duke basketball, Maple Leafs hockey, Notre Dame's Rudy and "Touchdown Jesus," and the fact that over 108 million people watched Jake Paul fight Mike Tyson (Chuck was there).

Sports are fueled by fandom.

---

[8] https://www.nytimes.com/2018/06/16/sports/world-cup/peru-denmark-russia.html

FANDOM HAS ALWAYS BEEN WITH US

We're not going to pretend that we did some extensive research project into the history and science of fandom. In an age of short attention spans, we know you probably wouldn't read it anyway. But here are some of the more interesting fandom factoids we stumbled across:

- Fandom releases pleasure chemicals like dopamine and oxytocin, which means it's borderline addictive!

JOHNNY, YOU'VE BEEN IN THERE FOR HOURS. ARE YOU WATCHING GATOR FOOTBALL AGAIN?

- There's evidence that sports fandom actually releases more endorphins than sex. In a 1997 University of Florida study,[9] researchers who showed subjects a variety of photographs while recording their physiological and subjective responses found that "extreme Gator sports fans" showed stronger positive reactions to pictures of Gator sporting events than to erotic pictures.

- "Fanatic" comes from the Latin *fanaticus*, which referred to people who went crazy for their gods. So yeah, fandom has been with us for a while.

- Our brains' mirror neuron system plays a key role in fandom because it allows us to empathize with others' emotions and actions. That's why a football team's victory feels like a

---

[9] https://archive.news.ufl.edu/articles/1997/05/uf-study-backs-suspicions-for-some-sports-really-is-better-than-sex.html

personal achievement, while a loss evokes genuine grief. (In Minnesota, it's mostly about the grief.)

The point is, before we apply "fandom" to franchising, we have to recognize that it's emotional, not rational. In sports, we essentially root for a uniform. Most of the players weren't born in our cities. We've never met them and likely never will. Vikings fans hated Brett Favre until he became our starting quarterback and started winning games. It doesn't make sense, yet it's a huge part of our lives and a multitrillion-dollar industry.

THE TRIBE HAS SPOKEN

At its core, fandom is about tribal identity. Whether it's actual tribes, sports fans or band groupies, we all express our fandom using shared elements: symbols (logos, colors, flags), a unique language ("I'm a Belieber"), rituals (games, concerts, annual conferences) and tribal stories (like this book).

What does the color purple mean to you? If you're from Minnesota, it's the Vikings, and it's Prince. But of course, for us it's mostly Anytime Fitness. We talk about "bleeding purple." Franchisees show up at our conferences with purple hair, purple shoes and, yes, purple tattoos.

But tribes are more than the sum of their parts. You can't just slap on the elements of tribalism and create one overnight. It has to happen organically, from the inside out, and your tribe has to have a larger meaning and purpose behind it.

Many franchisees say that the biggest value they receive isn't operational support; it's belonging to a community of like-minded entrepreneurs. These connections give them both practical advice and emotional sustenance unavailable to stand-alone business owners.

There's also "visceral tribalness." The most powerful tribes have a common enemy. You can't know what you stand for without knowing what you stand against, and there's a reason we didn't allow anyone at Anytime Fitness to wear red in our office (the primary brand color of a local competitor) during what we call the "copycat years" of 2003–2009.

But at the same time, we've always known that our true enemy has never been other gym franchises. In fact, we used to shock our franchisees by saying, "Hey, if a member decides to join another fitness club, congratulate them!" Our purpose is around health and well-being. Sedentary lifestyles, poor diet and lack of motivation are the real villains — not other businesses that stand in the arena with us.

FANDOM ON THE JOB: A RARE AND ENDANGERED SPECIES

Now that we've got you thinking about fandom, compare how you feel about your favorite musical artist or sports team to how you feel about your job. Chances are, it's not the same. Why is that?

Most of us work about 2,000 hours a year. We sleep about the same amount. That means we devote nearly 40% of our waking hours to an organization. *That's* the brand that truly dominates our lives. *That's* the community we spend most of our time with. *That's* where we should get a sense of purpose in our lives. Yet how many companies truly inspire passion?

If you bought into a franchise system, you've likely invested hundreds of thousands — maybe millions — of dollars into it. It's a hugely important part of your life. It puts food on your table. But ask yourself, "Am I a true *fan* of my franchise brand?" Be honest. Do you get as emotionally involved with your team of employees as you do with your favorite NFL or EPL[10] team? Probably not.

Anytime Fitness is known for the fandom we've inspired. That's why we have the credibility to write this book. Our conferences vibrate with energy and purpose. We and the people in our system — employees, franchisees, members, even vendors and suppliers — are known for wearing purple kilts, painting our faces and getting our logo tattooed onto our bodies.

That fandom has taken on a life of its own, but we'd like to think we've led by example. I mean, we love music and sports as much as anyone. But our colleagues, franchisees, partners, investors and members mean a billion times more to us than any game. Vikings purple is a fun diversion on a Sunday afternoon. Anytime Fitness purple pays for college educations, funds vacations and fills retirement accounts. When a Vikings game is over, it's over. We think about work 24/7 because we want to.

For most people, it's the opposite. And frankly, we don't get it. Why do we crank our sports and music fandom up to eleven, then turn the knob down to zero from 8 to 5? Because it's "unprofessional"? "Improper"? Are we not supposed to love what we do? We wrote *Love Work* on that topic because we can't imagine spending 2,000 hours a year on something we're not passionate about.

According to Gallup,[11] employee engagement in the U.S. recently fell to its lowest level in a decade, with only 31% of people feeling engaged with their jobs. That's less than a third of us feeling any sense of "fandom" in the workplace.

---

[10] That's "English Premier League" for our American readers (though the EPL is gaining more American fans all the time).

[11] https://www.gallup.com/workplace/654911/employee-engagement-sinks-year-low.aspx

Franchising is no exception, and it's time to change that. Will transforming your franchise into a *Fanchise* make it more successful and more valuable? Yes, but you know what's even better? It'll also make it a hell of a lot more fun.

FANCHISE "QUESTION & ACTION" ITEMS

For Franchisees

Question: Do you feel genuine pride in and connection to your brand, or is it just a paycheck?

> **Action**: Write down three ways your business positively impacts lives beyond just making money, then share them with your team.

Question: Are you creating a workplace where your employees feel they belong to a "tribe"?

> **Action**: Ask your team: *What makes you proud to work here?* Use their answers to shape your culture.

Question: Are you showing up as the biggest fan of your own business?

> **Action**: Lead by example: Wear the brand, tell its story and celebrate wins loudly.

For Franchisors

Question: Are you building a brand that people want to tattoo on their bodies?

> **Action**: Do a quick audit: What *specific rituals, symbols and stories* define your culture today?

Question: Are you inspiring franchisee emotional connection, or just compliance?

> **Action**: Spend a day with a franchisee and see your system through their eyes.

Question: Are you clear on who your "enemy" is, and are you rallying your team against it?

> **Action**: Define it explicitly and communicate it consistently.

[2]

FRANCHISES ARE MORE *FANCHISABLE* THAN OTHER BUSINESSES

"

Franchising is the world's most compelling business structure to allow people to be masters of their own destiny. When it works well, there's no better growth engine.

— Jim Goniea

"

> **"** Franchising allows people to go into business for themselves, but not by themselves. You've got people with skin in the game. When it's done right, there's something unique and special about it. **"**
>
> — Matt Haller

> **"** It's about relationships. If you have a model that works, and you can have good relationships, you can do really well in franchising. **"**
>
> — Joe Fittante

WHY ARE WE talking about fandom in the franchise space instead of at the general, stand-alone business level? Because it's what we know, sure. But it's also because franchising is a system that basically gives you a license to 3D-print passion.

With all due respect to the international audience (hopefully) reading this book, there's also something uniquely American about franchising. When Ben Franklin expanded his printing business, he gave his workers printing houses in other colonies and provided all their equipment in exchange for a third of the profits over six years.

The partners provided the labor. And at the end of their terms, they could purchase the equipment back from Franklin and work for themselves.

Sound familiar?

Fast-forward to Isaac Singer, who developed a franchise-like system to distribute and repair his Singer sewing machines in the mid-19th century. In the mid-20th century along come fast-food chains like McDonald's, as well as service-based franchises like Marriott. These businesses catapulted franchising into the stratosphere. Today, over 3,000 franchise concepts exist in the United States alone.[12]

THE PERFECT COMBINATION

Why did franchising take off as a business model? Because it sits at the intersection of big-brand *power* and small-business *heart*.

When you walk into a locally owned Anytime Fitness club — or hopefully any other franchise — you experience a magical combination: the consistency and trust of a global brand coupled with the passion and community connection of a local entrepreneur. It's the best of both worlds.

Franchising is built on win-win relationships. The franchisor provides the road map, tools and support. Franchisees bring the hustle, heart and local relationships. When both sides fulfill their end of the bargain, customers get an experience they can't stop talking about.

But there's also something deeper at work. The most successful franchisees and franchisors understand that the real magic happens when you're selling more than just a product or service; you're selling

---

[12] https://franchiselawyer.com/franchise-legal-resources/franchise-industry-facts

transformation. Whether it's helping someone get healthier, look better or simply feel more confident, transformation creates emotional connections that no marketing budget can buy.

And no one can scale that transformation like a franchise.

We've seen this firsthand for over two decades. When an Anytime Fitness franchisee helps one of their members feel better, go off their high-blood-pressure or diabetes meds, overcome their depression, or play with their kids or grandkids, that member doesn't just become a customer; they become an evangelist. And when a franchisee builds a thriving business that supports their family and community, they don't just become an operator; they become a true believer.

THE 3 STAGES OF FRANCHISE EVOLUTION

Anytime Fitness is a mature franchise, but it's important to remember that all franchise systems exist along a spectrum of size and maturity. It's helpful to break them down into three stages:

Stage 1: The Startup

At this early phase, the franchisor has an unproven concept and unproven ability to scale their franchise.

Stage 2: The Developing Franchise

At this stage, the franchisor has a semi-proven concept and the core elements to scale their system, including operations, marketing, finance, compliance, franchise development, construction and real estate.

Stage 3: The Mature Franchise

The franchisor has a proven concept, greater depth in the Stage 2 core elements, plus additional capabilities, a proven ability to scale and multi-unit operators.

Along this evolution, a successful franchise concept doesn't stay isolated or limited to one location for one audience. It's systematized, packaged and replicated across dozens, hundreds or thousands of locations. This creates multiple value streams flowing to everyone involved.

For franchisors, the math is compelling. A proven business model gets multiplied across locations without requiring the same capital investment that corporate expansion would demand. Each new franchise agreement generates initial fees, ongoing royalties and often additional revenue through supply chain relationships — all while the franchisee takes on their share of the financial risk and management.

For franchisees, the model is equally attractive. They get to be their own boss. They get access to a turnkey business system, complete with brand recognition, proven operations manuals, ongoing support and collective purchasing power. The risk of business failure — something that plagues most independent startups — is far lower.

In the franchise system versus stand-alone businesses, every franchise has some element of *Fanchise*-ness that can be built upon. We often say that the top 5–10% of revenue leaders in a franchise system simply do things at a higher level. Some amplify the most passion-inducing elements of the franchise brand; others create passion on their own within their unique communities.

When you ask a high performer for the best advice they can give to a new franchisee, it's often three simple words: "follow the model." They do that, and they also make the model better.

THE BOTTOM LINE: A MILLIONAIRE-MAKING MACHINE

❝

Do you have any idea how many millionaires Anytime Fitness has created in Australia alone? I did the math. It's at least 300!

— Richard Peil
Anytime Fitness Master Franchisee, Australia

❞

While entrepreneurs constantly search for the perfect way to achieve financial freedom, the franchise model has quietly but consistently delivered extraordinary results across industries, geographies and economic cycles. It's not an exaggeration to say that it's probably the world's greatest system for building wealth.

It's hard to measure, but we're confident that Anytime Fitness has created over 1,000 millionaires worldwide since its founding in 2002 (with memberships averaging only around $35/month). And we're not alone. From quick-service restaurants to home services, franchising has a unique ability to generate wealth for ordinary people without specialized skills or extraordinary capital. The Anytime Fitness brand has also generated millions of dollars for our vendors and suppliers (when you read about the creation of "purple turf" in Chapter 12, know that the manufacturer of that product has done very well for themselves).

Some of you reading this book already know the franchising fundamentals, but here's the nutshell version for those who don't:

1. **Operational Leverage.** Franchisees benefit from systems and processes refined through hundreds or thousands of locations. Those efficiencies flow directly to the bottom line.

2. **Brand Value.** Independent businesses have to build recognition from scratch. Franchisees can tap into established brands that attract customers from day one, dramatically lowering marketing costs and boosting revenue growth.

3. **Scalability.** The franchising model allows successful operators to expand to multiple units and grow their wealth exponentially. (Owning one Anytime Fitness club can generate a comfortable living. Owning 10 can create generational wealth.)

4. **Multiple Exit Strategies.** Successful franchisees have more options for monetizing their investment than independent business owners do. They can sell back to the franchisor, to other franchisees, to outside investors looking to join the system or (increasingly) to private-equity firms.

THE FOUNDER FACTOR

Unlike traditional corporations, where most CEOs and other executives remain distant figures, franchise systems often maintain direct connections between founders and franchisees. This accessibility creates a powerful personal connection. A franchise that

43

can trace its success to a founder's original vision can create fierce brand loyalty. But to create a *Fanchise*, founders need more than vision. They need unrivaled passion for and engagement with their brand.

THE FREEDOM FACTOR

> **"**
>
> **KOA's early franchisees were 'Fanchisees' because they were buying more than a way to make a living. They were buying a lifestyle. These are people who wanted to spend their lives camping, and KOA opened the door for them to do exactly that. "**
>
> — Chuck Modell

Of course, wealth isn't measured only in dollars. True wealth includes control over your time, a feeling of purpose in your work and freedom from unnecessary stress. Franchising delivers here too.

One of the strengths of the 24/7 Anytime Fitness model is the fact that it requires minimal staffing. Plus, owners are free to leave their clubs "anytime" and know that members can still work out. This translates to lower payroll and fewer management headaches than other franchise models. More importantly, it frees franchisees to live a more balanced life.

A naysayer might argue that franchising is actually the most difficult business model because more stakeholders are involved.

Every business has customers to serve, suppliers to work with and investors to make happy. But only franchising has the unique franchisor/franchisee relationship.

Does this create some challenges? Our attorney friends on both the franchisor and the franchisee sides of the fence would say "yes." But the opportunities far outweigh them. Brian Schnell routinely hands out cards identifying "The 5 Habits of Highly Successful Franchise Systems." His list echoes the values we planned to talk about in this book:

1. Maintain an undying devotion to the brand.

2. Balance the interests of all stakeholders.

3. Recruit top-quality franchisees.

4. Obsess over franchisee profitability.

5. Empower franchisees.

It's true: When these elements align, the wealth-building potential is extraordinary.

ROEI: RETURN ON EMOTIONAL INVESTMENT

> **One of our suppliers once told me, 'Sometimes I feel more like an Anytime Fitness employee than an employee of my actual company.' When suppliers are that emotionally invested, you know you've built something special.**
>
> — Libby Junker

We talked about this in *Love Work*, and it's worth revisiting here. In franchising, the profitability metrics are clear: unit sales, EBITDA, same-store growth, franchisee turnover rates. These numbers tell a compelling story of financial health and operational efficiency. But the most successful franchise systems understand that the most valuable metrics often don't appear on a spreadsheet.

In other words, even though there's no way to quantify it, franchising is by nature a more emotional space than other corporate industries. We coined the term ROEI (Return on Emotional Investment) to recognize that franchising's greatest strength is its people. Traditional ROI (Return on Investment) is an important metric, but we broke through the growth ceiling that still constrains some of our competitors when we shifted from viewing employees as a "cost center" to seeing them as assets worth investing in. (More on this in Chapter 10: "*Fanchise* Your Team.")

Most franchise systems are more enlightened than other businesses, but they can still underestimate the soft skills. Leaders don't go there because there's no way for them to measure things like "Number of Tears Shed During a Member Success Story." How do you quantify the ROI of franchisees telling you they've fallen in love with who they've become?[13] Or one club member donating a kidney to another?[14] Or a personal trainer quite literally saving a member's life by helping them overcome severe depression?[15]

If we tell our shareholders and board members that we "out-care the competition," they might look at us cross-eyed. But we're convinced that these emotional returns raise the multiple that a

---

[13] We've experienced this.
[14] This too.
[15] And this.

private-equity firm will pay for your business. In a competitive marketplace where business models are easily copied, the emotional bonds between franchisors, franchisees, employees and customers are the X factor.

GENERATIONAL WEALTH

More than other business models, franchising can create and sustain a family atmosphere. Many successful franchise systems have second- and third-generation franchisees — children who chose to follow their parents into the same brand family.

Ron Gardner points to KFC's strong family atmosphere. A large percentage of their franchisees are family operations that own three or fewer stores, and many of the owners grew up hanging out at the KFC conventions their parents attended. This doesn't happen nearly as often with non-franchise businesses.

In a world where business relationships are increasingly transactional, franchises create deeper emotional connections that transform ordinary brands into passionate communities. And *Fanchises* take them to the next level.

FANCHISE "QUESTION & ACTION" ITEMS

For Franchisees

Question: Are you taking full advantage of the systems and brand value your franchisor provides, or trying to go it alone?

> **Action**: Review your operations, compare them to the franchise playbook, and identify one area to improve or align more closely.

Question: Do you see your business as a platform to change lives, not just make sales?

> **Action**: Write down three ways you've helped transform customers' lives in the last month. Share one story publicly.

Question: Are you planning for the future by scaling your business and creating generational wealth?

> **Action**: Talk to your franchisor or mentor about multi-unit ownership and what it takes to grow responsibly.

For Franchisors

Question: Are you making "emotional connection" a measurable part of your brand culture?

> **Action**: Create a simple survey or feedback loop to capture "ROEI" moments from franchisees and customers each quarter.

Question: Are you balancing your own growth with franchisee profitability?

> **Action**: Run a quick analysis: Are your franchisees seeing healthy margins and sustainable growth?

Question: Are you empowering your franchisees to become raving fans of your brand?

> **Action**: Offer a platform for them to tell their transformation stories at conferences or in marketing materials.

[3]

FRANCHISING IS MORE *FANCHISABLE* TODAY THAN EVER

❝

There's more infrastructure around franchising today. You've got a founder. You've got mom-and-pop franchisees, but also multi-unit franchisees. You've got private-equity firms on both sides. You've got brokers, packaging firms, consultants. The relationships have definitely gotten more complicated. **❞**

— Matt Haller

TODAY, CHUCK MODELL is one of the world's most well-regarded franchise attorneys in a large and growing field. But back in the early 1980s, he was one of only a handful of lawyers at one of the early International Franchise Association annual meetings. Most of the attendees were franchisors — male CEOs and founders who were passionate about their businesses but had little need for legal counsel at industry events.

"I stood at the Fontainebleau Hotel in Miami trying to solicit business from these people for $80 an hour," Chuck says. "I'd approach franchisors in meetings — and at the bar — introduce myself as a franchise attorney and try to convince them I could help them. Most of them shot me a skeptical look and asked why a lawyer would even be at this conference. I was there to find new clients, but I was also learning the business side of franchising. My start-up and early-stage franchisor clients needed someone who could not only prepare their legal documents but also address their potential business issues."

Chuck Modell was way ahead of his time. We've now spoken at several IFA conventions, and today they're packed with thousands of lawyers, accountants, consultants, private-equity investors and suppliers. It's no longer a simple gathering of business owners, and franchising is no longer dominated by founders selling their proven systems to mom-and-pop operators. It's a sophisticated, multi-layered ecosystem with multiple stakeholders.

If you want to create a *Fanchise* within this complicated system, you have to surround yourself with suppliers and other partners who actually understand franchising — especially the unique relationship between franchisors and franchisees.

Case in point: We recently heard about a franchisor who required stores to adopt a new point of sale (POS) system. Some franchisees used it to create alternative pricing policies that went against the franchisor's policy manual. When the franchisor's president talked to the franchisees about it, he found that the POS vendor had recommended the changes because they generated extra income for *them*. The vendor didn't "get" the franchisor–franchisee relationship or the need for uniformity across a system. If they had truly understood franchising, none of this would have happened.

> **If you want to create a *Fanchise* ... you have to surround yourself with suppliers and other partners who actually understand franchising — especially the unique relationship between franchisors and franchisees.**

As part of this project, we asked our Expert Panel what's changed most in franchising over the last four decades. Their answers boiled down to six trends. While these changes have created some challenges, they've also opened up greater opportunities to transform a franchise into a *Fanchise* than ever before.

CHANGE #1: THE EXPLOSION OF PRIVATE-EQUITY INVESTMENT

This topic is so big that we gave it its own section later on (Chapter 9). But for now, let's just say that private-equity (PE) firms have become major players in franchising at both the franchisor and franchisee levels.

"On balance, the role of PE in franchising has been very good, but not in all instances," says Matt Haller. "Like with anything, there are good players and bad players."

In other words, while PE has brought in capital for technology, talent and infrastructure, it has also changed the dynamics of many franchise systems. Good PE partners understand the unique franchisor–franchisee relationship; others see franchising merely as a financial opportunity without appreciating its relational aspects.

As Jim Goniea puts it, "Some PE firms are into it for 20 fiscal quarters, tops. They want to extract value too early and for the wrong reasons."

"PE has provided valuable capital to help brands invest in technology and people," adds Matt Haller. "And it has brought a sense of financial prudence that some founders need."

CHANGE #2. THE GROWTH OF MULTI-UNIT, MULTI-BRAND OPERATORS

The traditional mom-and-pop, single-unit franchisee has evolved quite a bit over the years. Today, large "platform" operators own multiple units across multiple brands (sometimes called MUMBOs: Multi-Unit, Multi-Brand Operators).

Matt Haller notes that while this can create wealth, it can also complicate the "small-business story" of franchising: the fact that franchising allows moms and pops to achieve the American Dream. Scott Greenberg cautions about what he calls "Multi-Unit Derangement Syndrome," where franchisors are more focused on selling large territories than ensuring franchisee success.

CHANGE #3. THE RISE OF CONSULTANTS, BROKERS AND PACKAGERS

Franchising used to be intimate enough that it didn't attract the classic "middlemen" that creep into most industries. But because the model has been so successful and created so much wealth, we've now seen explosive growth in third-party consultants, brokers and packaging firms.

These entities exist to help businesses transform into franchises and help potential franchisees find opportunities, but the incentives aren't always aligned. As Joe Fittante notes,

I can take you worldwide for just $150,000!

"Franchisors and franchisees don't always know who they're getting into bed with."

These intermediaries can add value, but when they're paid on commission rather than outcomes, they also add risk. If you tell a small-business owner that you can turn their business into a franchise, then walk away after the papers are signed, you're not invested in long-term success. Plus, many successful businesses simply aren't ready for franchising, and some never will be.

CHANGE #4: MORE REGULATORY SCRUTINY

Franchising faces more regulatory challenges than ever before. Some of this comes from a misperception that the franchisor—

franchisee dynamic is some kind of David-and-Goliath, "powerful vs. powerless" relationship. In other cases, it's a natural consequence of a minority of bad actors doing franchising the wrong way, or aggressive labor unions targeting franchising as their own growth opportunity.

Unfortunately, the franchise industry now suffers through the same whiplash political cycles as so many other industries. Wild swings from one end of the spectrum to the other have a way of eroding stability, which is never a winning strategy.

CHANGE #5: INTERNATIONAL EXPANSION

Franchises increasingly expand beyond their countries of origin. Anytime Fitness is a prime example, growing from one Midwestern club to operations across 42 countries on all seven continents. This international growth has created new opportunities, but it has also created challenges in translating brand values across cultures.

Successful Global *Fanchises* are able to" glocalize": maintain core brand values while adapting to local cultures and markets. (More on this in Chapter 12.)

CHANGE #6: TECHNOLOGY

Technology has changed every industry, so what's unique about franchising? First, the scale. Nearly half of Anytime Fitness corporate employees now serve in technological roles. Half! We wouldn't be surprised if most franchise businesses are seeing the same thing, regardless of industry.

Second, the growing importance of technology only bolsters the case for why franchising is such a powerful business model. If you're looking to start a business, you have two choices: Stay independent and try to keep up with innovations on your own, or join a franchise system with the built-in capability to support technological evolutions and revolutions — efficiently and at scale.

Are all of these changes favorable for franchisees and franchisors? No, but their net effect is to make *Fanchising* easier and more necessary than ever before.

FANCHISE "QUESTION & ACTION" ITEMS

For Franchisees

Question: Are you selecting partners and consultants based on long-term value rather than short-term promises?

> **Action**: Vet all third-party advisors for both experience and alignment with your goals and values. Avoid those who are likely to disappear after the initial sale.

Question: Are you building your business with a long-term mindset, not just chasing short-term wins?

> **Action**: Attend an IFA conference or other industry event to expand your knowledge and network.

Question: Are you ready for the increased role of technology in your business?

> **Action**: Set a goal to master one new tool or system this year that your franchisor offers. Ask for training if you feel behind.

For Franchisors

Question: From PE to multi-unit operators, are you selecting the *right* partners, who align with your values?

Action: Establish criteria for partnerships that emphasize cultural fit as much as capital.

Question: Are you protecting your brand from brokers, packagers or consultants who don't have skin in the game?

Action: Make sure all your intermediaries have clear accountability tied to franchisee success, not just signing deals.

Question: Are you keeping your system "glocal" as you expand internationally?

Action: Gather input from local franchisees in each market to ensure your core values resonate culturally.

PART II:

START
FANCHISING
NOW

[4]

LEARN YOUR *FANCHISE* FUNDAMENTALS

"

[T]hroughout the good-to-great companies, passion became a key part of the Hedgehog Concept. You can't manufacture passion or 'motivate' people to feel passionate. You can only discover what ignites your passion and the passions of those around you. **"**

— Jim Collins, *Good to Great*

A *FANCHISABLE* PRODUCT & CULTURE

From Chuck:

IT'S A GORGEOUS Minnesota afternoon in July 2009, and for some reason I find myself sitting on horseback in a purple kilt and a long wig. Dave is next to me in a similar and equally ridiculous costume.

We've pulled dozens of our employees away from their desks to film a daylong parody video in the middle of the workweek. And as we wait for the director to yell "action," I can't help but calculate the expense of this venture in my head, wonder how we'll ever recoup the investment and question the decisions that have led to this moment.

We're making "Saveheart," a parody of *Braveheart*, for our upcoming annual franchisee conference. The plot is simple: Dave and I are leading the brave warriors of Anytime Fitness, dressed in white T-shirts emblazoned with words like "Passion," "Determination" and "Energy," against the insidious enemy forces of "Pizza," "Diabetes," "Apathy" and others. In

Dave, this is either the best or the worst idea we've ever had.

one of the more subtle jokes, each tribe has someone identified as "Six Pack" (as in "beer" and "abs").

Like any video production, it's a long, tedious, start-and-stop process. Lots of footage to cover. Lots of waiting. Lots of sun, and lots of sweat. When you're making a video like this, you have no idea whether it's going to win an Oscar or be a total embarrassment. I'm worried that it's going to be the latter, at a cost in production and lost productivity in the tens of thousands of dollars.

But then something happens. Instead of our team goofing off or getting bored, they grow more and more passionate about the fake battle they're fighting. Why? Because it resembles the *actual* battle they fight every day. It's why they get up in the morning, and it's why they do everything they can to help our franchisees succeed. People from different departments are laughing together and bonding over this bizarre yet meaningful shared experience.

In the final scene, the exhausted heroes of Anytime Fitness claim victory and shout "Freedom!" "Anytime!" "Fitness!" over the "dead" bodies of their enemies. And they really mean it.

Dave & Chuck spoofing Braveheart in "Saveheart."

A few months later, *Saveheart* is a huge hit at our conference. Franchisees in the audience shout "Freedom!" "Anytime!" "Fitness!" unprompted, and a tribe is born.

"Freedom! Anytime! Fitness!"

The impact of this experience reverberated far beyond that summer day. Employees still reference it. Franchisees still break into the "freedom" chant at conferences. And the purple kilts remain a symbol of our tribal passion and fight

to make all of our stakeholders fall in love with their new, healthier and happier selves.

Whether you're a franchisee or franchisor, you can focus on your culture when you already have an excellent product to build a franchise around. With Anytime Fitness, we essentially landed on a Hedgehog Concept before we knew that Jim Collins had created that idea in *Good to Great*. This concept is essentially about focus (which hedgehogs have) and finding the sweet spot between three things: 1) what you're deeply passionate about, 2) what you can be the best in the world at, and 3) what drives your economic or resource engine.

The original Anytime Fitness Hedgehog Concept looked like the diagram below. We were passionate about fitness. We were best at making it convenient, accessible and affordable. And our economic engine was recurring revenue, reduced payroll and operational simplicity. We created a compact club with just the cardio and weight equipment that most people wanted, and we gave our members 24/7 access to it.

Anytime Fitness
Original Hedgehog Concept

Passionate About
(Fitness)

Best At
(Convenience)

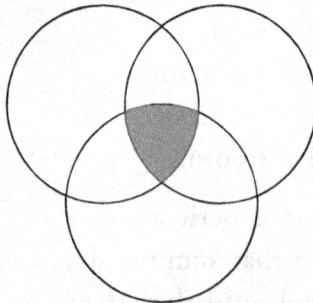

Economic Engine
(Cardio & Weights 24/7)

But as we mentioned earlier, even the best Hedgehog Concept needs to evolve and adapt. Ours was original but easily copied. Snag 5,000 square feet of space in a strip mall? Check. Load it with weights and cardio equipment? Easy. Give everyone 24/7 access? No problem. What's so special about that?

We spent years telling our team, "Look, every fitness franchise out there is trying to acquire and retain members. We all have the same equipment. We all have the same strategic plan. It's *how* we do it that makes the difference. How fast can we work together? How well can we work together? How well can we work with our Franchise Advisory Council? Are we truly collaborative?

Our real intellectual property has always been our culture, a level of *caring* that can't be measured. Some franchise brands are precious about their product; we've always been precious about our culture. The hard work of making Anytime Fitness a sustained success was tapping that culture to evolve our concept and stay ahead of the copycats.

Thanks to our stakeholders' combined efforts, we kept growing while most of the copycats faded away. Why? Because our culture was obsessed with helping franchisees help their members, and our franchisees were willing to evolve *with* us as we added tools like technology, coaching and personal training to stay ahead of the curve.

Lots of books have been written about creating a franchisable product, then optimizing your operations to make it successful. We never intended this book to be about the product, but we also don't want to gloss over its importance. Whether you're a franchisee or franchisor, none of our guidance will work if the market doesn't see value in your product or service. Even if they do, you have to keep making it better.

The goal of a *Fanchise* is to have a rock-solid product that frees you to focus on culture.

FANCHISE YOURSELF FIRST

> **When we love something, emotion often drives our actions. This is the gift and the challenge entrepreneurs face every day: The companies we dream of and build from scratch are part of us, and intensely personal. They are our families, our lives.**
>
> — Howard Schultz, *Onward*

It might sound obvious, but one of our *Fanchise* fundamentals corresponds to the first circle in Jim Collins' Hedgehog Concept: "What are you passionate about?" We'll help you remember it with a tongue-twister:

Fandom flows from founders to franchisees.

Howard Schultz's passion moment came on a 1983 trip to Milan, where he first experienced the magic of Italy's coffeehouses. He was already working at Starbucks, and he loved its coffee. But Italy made him fall in love with coffee *culture*, and that's a different animal. He started his own Italian-style coffee shop before returning to Starbucks to lead that company, and the rest is history.

Anita Roddick found her inspiration in a passion for the environment and empowering women. She saw other cosmetic products designed to make women look a certain way using excessive packaging. Determined to help women be the best versions of themselves, she channeled that passion into the first Body Shop store in Brighton, England, in 1976 — selling ethically sourced products with natural ingredients from around the world in refillable packaging.

Kristina Butler had her passion moment in 1998 while working as a registered nurse in home health care. After realizing that her patients valued companionship even more than medical care, she founded Comfort Keepers, which now makes a huge difference in the lives of seniors and other adults in over 700 locations in 13 countries.

As we documented in *Love Work*, our passion for health and fitness runs deep, and it's personal. Chuck lost his brother Steve to a heart condition at the age of 18, giving him a unique perspective on how lucky most of us are to be born with a healthy body (and how we should keep it that way). While living with his brother in Minot, North Dakota, Dave learned the value of empathy and mentoring when his wrestling coach would buy him a burger after practice because he suspected he wasn't getting enough to eat at home.

These experiences, and those of so many other franchise founders, have allowed people over the decades to *Fanchise* themselves before starting their own *Fanchises*. The same principle applies at the franchisee level, where we've seen hundreds of Anytime Fitness club owners leave their previous jobs and careers behind and find true passion in helping their neighbors and communities get healthier.

> **"Chuck lost his brother Steve to a heart condition at the age of 18, giving him a unique perspective on how lucky most of us are to be born with a healthy body. While living with his brother in Minot, North Dakota, Dave learned the value of empathy and mentoring when his wrestling coach would buy him a burger after practice because he suspected he wasn't getting enough to eat at home."**

FANCHISING IS "NATION BUILDING"

Deep in the Amazon rainforest, you'll find a group known as the Yanomamis. They've been isolated from other people for thousands of years, so they've developed a unique culture. They live in circular communal houses called yanos. Their languages have no known relatives. They count moons instead of months. Instead of years, they track the harvests of the pupunha fruit.

How do we know this? We Googled it! Did we mention that there isn't a college degree between the two of us? Anyway ...

While a franchise business isn't exactly an indigenous tribe, the hallmark of a *Fanchise* is its unique cultural traits. The franchise coaching system known as EOS, the Entrepreneurial Operating System, is a perfect example. In addition to its orange color, it thrives on its unique language. Terms like Visionary, Implementer, IDS,

Rock, Scorecard and Clarity Break are unique to the business, and many of them are now trademarked.

Chick-fil-A restaurants are known for saying "my pleasure" in response to any "thank you" from a customer; for being closed on Sundays, merging Southern hospitality (and food) with Christian values; and for prohibiting franchisees (or "operators") from owning multiple units so they can provide exceptional service at each location.

While not a franchise, Salesforce and its annual Dreamforce events are another great example. Dreamforce draws over 100,000 attendees from over 100 countries, making it one of the largest tech conferences in the world. On paper, Salesforce is "just" a CRM. But to its community of fans, it's a culture unto itself.

Anytime Fitness has its own language and colors. We "bleed purple." We hold our franchisees to our PLEASE standards (Personal, Listen, Empathy, Anticipate Needs, Sense of Urgency and Encouragement). There's the tattoo thing. When we talk to other business leaders, especially in franchising, we ask, "What's the language that only *you* know? What's something specific to your brand that you can't find anywhere else?" If an outsider wades into your culture, you want them to think, *I don't get it, but I love it!*

When outsiders attend our Anytime Fitness conferences, they're amazed at the unique culture that bombards their senses. The purple. The music. The Runningman logo. The kilts from "Saveheart." As you'll see in many of the email messages we share in this

Our AF corporate staff gearing up (and getting tribal) for a themed event at one of our conferences

book, Dave and I sometimes refer to our staff as "Sherpas," because we walk with people on their journeys, carry some of their weight and help them achieve their climb in business and life.

The point is, your *Fanchise* can't be generic. If you want to build one from scratch or transform your current business into one, you have to think of it as nation building.

FANCHISING IN ANY INDUSTRY

> **The point is not what core values you have, but that you have core values at all, that you know what they are, that you build them explicitly into the organization, and that you preserve them over time. Enduring great companies preserve their core values and purpose while their business strategies and operating practices endlessly adapt to a changing world.**
>
> — Jim Collins, *Good to Great*

As we've talked about passion and purpose over the years, a common counterargument we've heard (and addressed in *Love Work*) is "That's easy for you guys to say. You're in the health and fitness space!" In other words, how can you create a *Fanchise* when the product or service you sell doesn't come with built-in emotion?

One way to clear this hurdle is to focus not on the specific product or service you sell but on the impact you make. In the movie *It's a Wonderful Life*, George Bailey gets to see what Bedford Falls would look like if he'd never been born. Do the same thing with your franchise business. What would happen if you didn't exist? Who would it impact, and how? Where would your employees be working today? How would their families be doing? How many college tuition payments would go unpaid, family trips never taken?

On paper, Red Bull is just another caffeinated beverage, but it has famously associated itself with extreme sports and "giving you wings." Nike was originally just another shoe brand until its "Just Do It" campaign made it synonymous with grit and determination. Sweetgreen could be seen as just another quick-serve, fast-casual restaurant, but it smartly attached itself to the bigger mission of "connecting people to real food."

No matter what it actually sells, any business can connect people to something greater. But most important is how you support your community at the individual-unit level. We've always seen a clear difference between the Anytime Fitness clubs that get involved in their communities and those that don't. The "success" and "community involvement" connection is so strong that we always recognize the most community-engaged gyms at every conference.

At the franchisee and franchisor levels, put company resources into contributions, volunteerism and mentoring. Not only do these efforts make communities better, but they also improve your value proposition, help you attract and retain better people, boost employee (and consumer) engagement, reduce the costs of turnover, and fuel growth.

Remember: Charities and nonprofits need more than money. They need volunteers, donated goods and in-kind services. Your expertise in marketing, technology, legal or accounting services can help them run better. And in helping them fulfill their purpose, you'll also fulfill your own. (More on this in Chapter 10.)

RECOGNIZE YOUR OWN *FANCHISE* MOMENTS[16]

Even though we're writing this book, we didn't set out to create a *Fanchise* with Anytime Fitness from day one. It happened organically because of who we are and what we were passionate about. But a critical element along the way was recognizing when the *Fanchise* revealed itself to us, then building on those moments.

The more notable ones include the following:

- During Anytime Fitness's first annual conference in August 2005, a member named Pat Welsh took the stage to share his success story. As he told the audience of 130 club owners, eyes watering and hands trembling, how working with a personal trainer helped him lose 100 pounds and regain his self-esteem, there wasn't a dry eye in the house. Today, we solicit Member Success Stories from around the world and turn many into high-quality videos that show the purpose behind the brand.

- At that same conference, a Russian immigrant and franchise owner named Mike Gelfgot spontaneously decided to get a tattoo of our Runningman logo on his left arm. Before long, we were offering free tattoos at our annual conferences. We now estimate that over 4,000 employees, franchisees, members, vendors and personal trainers now sport Runningman tattoos across the globe.

- As we mentioned earlier, at our 2009 annual conference in Atlanta, we put on our purple kilts, showed "Saveheart" and were blown away to hear franchisees spontaneously repeat the

---

[16] A moment that makes you realize you've created more than just a business; you've created a *Fanchise* that has taken on a life of its own.

chant at the end of the video. We still look back on that experience as a key turning point in transforming from a franchise into a *Fanchise*.

- At our 2016 conference in Lake Placid, NY, we set two Guinness records: one when more than 1,200 franchisees and staff performed squats together for one minute (nearly doubling the previous record of 665); and again when 1,200+ people did jumping jacks simultaneously for one minute (beating the prior record of 900).

- When Anytime Fitness club owner Anna Dey married her sweetheart, Mike, at the summit of Mount Kilimanjaro, they celebrated by raising a purple Anytime Fitness flag there. Similar flags have now been raised on Mount Rainier, Machu Picchu and Mount Everest.

Have you experienced moments like these? Have you ever gotten a sneak peek at the true potential of your business to connect with people, improve communities and change the world? Once you become a *Fanchise*, you'll experience them all the time. And you'll never want them to stop.

FANCHISE "QUESTION & ACTION" ITEMS

For Franchisees

Question: Do you know your numbers as well as your franchisor does?

> **Action:** Set aside time this week to review key performance metrics (revenue, retention, member satisfaction) and identify one area for improvement.

Question: Are you consistently executing the basics before chasing new ideas?

> **Action:** Audit your daily operations to ensure that the fundamentals (service quality, cleanliness, staffing) are flawless before adding complexity.

Question: Do you understand your franchisor's playbook and follow it?

> **Action:** Revisit your operations manual and training notes to refresh your knowledge of the core model.

For Franchisors

Question: Have you clearly defined the non-negotiable fundamentals for your system?

> **Action**: Create a simple checklist of the 5–7 key operational standards every franchisee must master.

Question: Are you tracking the right KPIs to monitor brand health?

> **Action**: Review your system-wide reporting to ensure you're measuring both financial and cultural indicators.

Question: Do you reinforce the basics in every interaction?

> **Action**: Use calls, conferences and communications to celebrate franchisees who excel at the fundamentals — not just those who break records.

[5]

FANCHISE YOUR PERSONAL PARTNERSHIPS

WE'VE BEEN BUSINESS partners and friends for 36 years, so we know a little something about successful partnerships. Our biggest test came in 2009.

At that time, Anytime Fitness was growing externally but battling internally. The company had three founders, and prior to starting Anytime Fitness, we'd been business partners in owning health clubs and a membership marketing company. We'd always found a way to make it work, but our challenges usually stemmed from a lack of alignment around long-term strategies and values.

As Anytime Fitness quickly grew to hundreds of locations in just a few years, those cracks only grew. Our other partner was in a different phase in life. His thinking was more short-term and shareholder-focused. We were more stakeholder-focused. We had a long-term vision for the brand, and we wanted to invest in capabilities that would help our franchisees run even more profitable clubs. Finally, in December 2009, we found a way to buy our third partner out. It was the biggest financial risk of our lives. But in the long run, it proved to be one of our best decisions.

When it was over, the two of us met on a quiet holiday weekday in the office for one of our "coffee talks." This has been a morning ritual for most of our partnership. We'll talk life, kids, sports, politics, religion and current events, but we'll eventually turn to the business. And we don't waste time basking in our success. We cover problems, opportunities and areas to improve, and we usually work ourselves into a frenzy with just how badly some areas of our business are performing.

During this particular coffee chat, we talked about our new partnership. We'd experienced our share of tense moments over the previous seven years. Now, with just the two of us, it was a time to rewire how we wanted to work together and where we wanted the company to go.

People who know us know how competitive we are. Anyone who has ever played Chuck in ping-pong knows that "hating to lose" is an understatement. We're talking Michael Jordan–level psychosis here. So during our third cup of black, bold coffee, we posed this question to ourselves:

> *If we were in a competition for Best Partnership,*
> *what would we do to make sure we won?*

Dave sipped his coffee and said, "Business partnerships are judged on the success of the business, so if we want to win, the business has to always come first."

And with that, we started drafting our Three Golden Rules of Partnership:

RULE #1: STAKEHOLDERS OVER SHAREHOLDERS

The business comes first. It's more important than either one of us. In franchising, a successful business means franchisees are operating profitable stores. Therefore, we would put franchisees before us. This rule would keep our egos in check because it's not about who has the better idea or who's right in an argument. In the end, the only thing that matters is if the business and franchisees are winning.

As the company grew and we created our parent company (Self Esteem Brands, now Purpose Brands), our vision became "to improve the self-esteem of the world." We included members as a critical stakeholder, so we would now serve member health on par with franchisee success.

RULE #2: TRUST THE OTHER'S INTENT

We committed to always listening to each other's points of view, challenging each other while also being open to being challenged (this evolved into Communication, Alignment and Trust, which we'll talk more about later).

We made sure we had strategic and cultural alignment on objectives and company values, which would develop into the 4 Ps of People, Purpose, Profits and Play. And we promised to trust the other's intentions. We have different leadership styles, but we know that our partner is always trying to make the company better.

RULE #3: TAKE THE WORK SERIOUSLY, NOT YOURSELF

We're naturally playful guys, and we love to "take the piss out of each other" (and others). Not taking ourselves too seriously would be another way to keep our egos in check, while also encouraging vulnerability, humility and approachability. If we could keep making fun of ourselves and each other, then other people would relate to us, and we'd be able to sustain a culture of collaboration, curiosity and fun.

THE HEAD & THE HEART

We had the unique opportunity to film an episode of the show *Secret Millionaire* in the summer of 2011. In part because we were deprived of technology and other distractions, we learned something new and profound about our partnership as we lived in a rundown house in Oklahoma City: Our secret weapon is that we approach leadership in different ways. Dave is "heart first." He feels something first, then it travels up to his brain. Chuck is "brain first," or more cerebral. He thinks first, then feels.

When choosing a business partner in franchising, bringing different strengths together creates a more complete leadership dynamic. We've seen partnerships fail because both people thought exactly alike, or because they couldn't respect each other's different approaches. In our case, Chuck analyzes the data and sees the logical path forward, while Dave feels the pulse of our franchisees and knows what will resonate in their hearts.

Together, we can speak to both the head and the heart of our business, and that creates the trust and alignment that builds and sustains our *Fanchise*.

LONG TERM VS. SHORT TERM

If there's a theme that runs through everything you read in this book, it's the importance of playing the long game. In theory, favoring the long term over the short term is easy. In practice, it's incredibly hard.

Every franchisor and franchisee wants to build a great brand. But well before they've achieved that, many feel compelled to buy their dream home and start rewarding themselves for their hard work. It's an understandable impulse, but it's also the quickest path to *Fanchise* failure.

Throughout the movie *It's a Wonderful Life*,[17] George Bailey faces choices around leaving Bedford Falls to travel and live his dream life (short term) or staying behind to help his partners, which are his family and community (long term). He always chooses to stay, and even though he faces incredible challenges, in the end he's hailed as "the richest man in town."

Committing to building a *Fanchise* means being willing to invest in all of your partnerships, and that means postponing your short-term desires over and over again. We've heard far too many stories about people, especially franchisors, who believed in long-term partnerships in theory, but not in practice.

The world of franchising is littered with businesses that were worth millions of dollars until their leaders chose quick personal gratification over long-term partnership investments, failed, then were sold for pennies on the dollar.

As we'll explore in Chapter 7, these same principles apply to the franchisor–franchisee relationship.

---

[17] Chuck loves this movie, so we reference it a lot.

FANCHISE "QUESTION & ACTION" ITEMS

For Franchisees

Question: Do you trust the intent of your franchisor's decisions, even when you don't fully agree with them?

> **Action:** Instead of defaulting to skepticism, ask clarifying questions to better understand the reasoning behind a decision before forming an opinion.

Question: Are you investing enough in your own staff, vendor and community partnerships to build long-term stability?

> **Action:** Choose one relationship to strengthen this month through proactive communication, shared goals or collaboration on a new initiative.

Question: Are short-term desires pulling resources away from long-term goals?

> **Action:** Review recent spending or time commitments and redirect one short-term indulgence toward something that will strengthen your business five years from now.

For Franchisors

Question: Are you putting stakeholders (franchisees, members, employees) ahead of shareholders and personal gain?

>   **Action**: Identify one decision this quarter where you can prioritize long-term brand health and franchisee profitability over short-term financial rewards.

Question: Do you and your leadership partners trust each other's intent, even when you disagree?

>   **Action**: Schedule a dedicated "alignment conversation" to revisit your shared vision, values and strategic priorities. Ensure you're both still on the same page.

Question: Is ego or the need to be "right" getting in the way of better solutions?

>   **Action**: In your next disagreement, focus entirely on the question "what's best for the business and franchisees?" rather than on who originated the idea.

[6]

FANCHISE EVERY STAKEHOLDER

"

If I only had 30 words in which to share my message instead of 80,000, it would be this: If you want to run a successful franchise business, keep a clear head, stick to the proven system and use your business to improve the lives of everyone it touches.

— Scott Greenberg

"

ON DECEMBER 17, 2024, we literally and figuratively passed the baton to a new CEO at Purpose Brands, Tom Leverton.

In addition to inscribing an actual baton, we wrote a love letter to staff that ended up being one of the most shared items we've ever created. Though we hadn't yet coined the term *"Fanchise,"* that spirit was clear:

Literally passing the baton to Purpose Brands CEO Tom Leverton, December 2024

If you want to be truly successful in franchising, you need to balance and meet the needs of every stakeholder, not just some of them.

> *To: Purpose Brand Staff*
>
> *From: Chuck & Dave*
>
> *Subject: Passing the Baton*
>
> *It's time.*
>
> *After 23 years of leading Self Esteem Brands, Dave and I are excited to pass the baton to a new CEO and talented leadership team at Purpose Brands. We've impacted millions of lives across 50 countries. Now these brands are well positioned to accelerate their growth, develop new services, and provide more robust support to the millions of members and thousands of franchise owners around the world.*
>
> *As founders, we've instilled our companies with a culture of how to think, care and win. Because it's not what we*

do that makes us special; it's how we do it. Which is why we're literally passing the baton with the following guiding principles:

Stakeholder First

Franchisees invest their hard-earned money, time, passion and dreams, and the weight of those responsibilities can only be carried by a deeply talented team of purpose-driven leaders who understand the formula for successful franchising: Shareholders' success follows stakeholders' success. If you make members and franchisees happy and successful, the brand grows and everyone wins.

Be the Reason It Works

Selfless leaders measure success by helping others achieve health and wealth. That's why we empower, recognize, and reward franchisees and employees with opportunities, resources and clear, accountable metrics to drive meaningful impact.

People, Purpose, Profits, Play

This has been our formula for a creating high-performance teams: We commit to a culture of uncommon care for PEOPLE, a clear and inspiring PURPOSE, driving stakeholder PROFITS, and fostering innovation and collaboration with a sense of childlike PLAY.

Be Humble, Bold and Curious

Traversing an uncertain and complex future requires a team that's willing to exercise intellectual humility — to challenge, debate, and leave room for new ideas and solutions. To go forward with courage, confidence and a bold mindset, and to listen, ask questions and approach life with endless curiosity.

Earned, Not Given

At the heart of everything we do is the belief that success is earned, not given. You can't create something of value without gritty effort, collaboration and an unrelenting drive. Remain committed to always learning, always earning!

This transition comes at the perfect time. We've recorded record highs in territory sales, revenue and EBITDA, finishing the year with over 5,800 clubs and studios open across 42 countries and seven continents.

We've achieved positive same-store sales across 90%+ of our global network, along with strong, collaborative relationships with franchisees. We're providing a new CEO with a tenured and talented leadership team. And best of all, more growth opportunities lie ahead as we pass the baton forward into a very exciting future.

To our millions of members worldwide, your journey has been our source of inspiration. We're obsessed with helping you be the very best you. Anyone. Anytime. Anywhere.

To the thousands of franchisees and master franchisees around the world, we admire your leadership, resourcefulness and purpose-driven risk-taking. By working together, we've made the world a healthier place one member, one club and one community at a time.

To our thousands of vendors and supplier team partners, thank you for supporting our franchisees with excellent products and first-class service — and for having fun with us along the way.

To the thousands of current and past employees over the last two decades, you've left us with internal tattoos of gratitude, memories, and a remarkable climb filled with personal and professional growth.

We've laughed and cried together, sweated together, challenged each other, inspired each other and made each other better. In turn, we've accomplished things no one could have ever imagined or thought possible. And we've done it the right way — fueled by a profound purpose to lift others.

Forever Grateful

Forever Inspired

Forever Forward

Dave Mortensen & Chuck Runyon

91

THE NEW FRANCHISE ECOSYSTEM

Forty-five years ago, Chuck Modell asked a law clerk to research all the franchise cases he could find. The resulting document was barely an inch thick. Today, those same case files fill three shelves in his office.

This physical growth perfectly illustrates the evolution of the franchise ecosystem. What began as a relatively straightforward relationship between franchisors and franchisees has transformed into a complex web of stakeholders, each with their own interests and incentives.

In the early days, franchise relationships were direct: A founder with a successful business model would sell franchises to mom-and-pop entrepreneurs looking to "be in business *for* themselves, but not *by* themselves." The franchisor provided the proven system. The franchisee provided the local knowledge and hustle. Together, they served the customer.

As we touched on in Chapter 3, today's franchise landscape looks dramatically different:

Private Equity (PE) has entered the scene on both sides of the equation. PE firms invest in franchisors, sometimes emphasizing short-term gains over long-term relationships. Meanwhile, PE is increasingly backing multi-unit franchisees, creating larger, more sophisticated operators with different needs than traditional mom-and-pop owners.

Brokers and Consultants now act as intermediaries between potential franchisees and franchisors. While they can provide valuable matchmaking services, their commission-based compensation model can put their incentives at odds with franchisees' long-term success.

Packagers are typically consultants or firms that promise to help business owners turn their existing business into a franchise system. They develop and assemble the components needed to franchise a business, effectively "packaging" it for replication, but they often make promises without properly preparing the business owner on what becoming a franchisor really entails.

International Expansion adds layers of master franchisees and cultural complexity to the system, requiring adaptability and nuance while you try to maintain brand consistency and integrity.

Legal Infrastructure has exploded. Specialized franchisee attorneys and increasing polarization create more disputes and regulatory scrutiny than ever before.

Technology is so important that a huge percentage of corporate staff are dedicated to some form of tech support.

This expanded ecosystem has opened up tremendous growth opportunities, but it has also created more potential points of friction. *Fanchises* navigate this complexity by remembering a fundamental truth: When stakeholders' interests align, the ecosystem thrives, regardless of how many players are involved.

A BALANCING ACT

> **All franchisees think about their work. Top franchisees work on how they think. That's their edge.**
>
> — Scott Greenberg

"Be obsessed with the consumer" is a common mantra in business. That's what Amazon and Apple are known for, right? It sounds good on the surface, but franchising is a different beast. Franchisees must focus on their customers. Franchisors must focus on their franchisees. And both need to focus on their employees, suppliers and investors. Every second of every day, every person in a leadership position has to decide: *Who gets the resources? Who gets the attention?*

Here's the uncomfortable truth of franchising that most leaders avoid talking about: When you have multiple stakeholders, you can't make everyone happy all the time. Someone will always feel shortchanged.

Our response to that is to avoid the adversarial, zero-sum-game mindset that too many franchise systems have. We strive to balance competing interests and ensure that each stakeholder sees a path forward. It ain't easy.

4 WAYS A *FANCHISE* NAVIGATES THE CHALLENGES OF MULTIPLE STAKEHOLDER INTERESTS

1. **A *Fanchise* obsesses over profitability.** On both the franchisor and franchisee levels, profits make big problems become small problems. The lack of it turns small problems into existential threats. Like a healthy tree, profitability creates oxygen for growth, innovation and collaboration.

2. **A *Fanchise* recognizes that few things build trust better and faster than transparency.** When we needed to increase technology fees at Anytime Fitness, we didn't just announce it, we explained why we were doing it, showed the ROI and gathered feedback. The franchisees who felt heard were more likely to accept the change, even if they didn't love it.

3. **A *Fanchise* remembers that trust doesn't mean avoiding conflict.** Encourage healthy tension. When our Franchise Advisory Council pushed back on a product launch, we paused, incorporated their feedback and relaunched nine months later. The result was stronger because it took everyone's perspectives into account.

4. **A *Fanchise* approaches every conversation from a stakeholder-first (not shareholder-first) mentality.** When making decisions, we always ask, "How does this benefit our members? How does this benefit the people who invest in owning our gyms?"

When conflicts arise, tackle them directly and with empathy. As we wrote in a 2010 email to our team:

"

We can't lose our empathy. We can't let it become 'us versus them.' Most of our franchisees know this, too, but that doesn't take away the emotions of the situation. We need to recognize their emotions by listening, understanding and providing empathy.

"

Remember: In building a *Fanchise*, you need every stakeholder to win enough to stay in the game, even if no one gets everything they want. Dave calls this "not everyone can win, but no one should lose."

ARE YOUR STAKEHOLDERS WINNING?

We're both longtime Minnesota Timberwolves season ticket holders. In fact, we have the best (and most expensive) piece of real estate at the Target Center: four courtside seats next to the visitors' bench. When you watch a Wolves game on TV, you'll likely see us cheering on our favorite NBA team while sitting next to whoever our archenemy is for that night.

The Timberwolves formed back in 1989, but only 13 of their 36 seasons to date have ended with more wins than losses. They turned things around in 2024 and 2025, becoming one of the most entertaining NBA teams to watch. They reached the Western Conference finals both years, and we can tell you from personal experience that few things can match the energy and intensity of NBA playoff basketball — even when your dreams are eventually shattered by the Dallas Mavericks or the Oklahoma City Thunder.

During all those losing Timberwolves seasons, we could barely give away our tickets to employees, friends and family members when we couldn't use them. But over the last two seasons, we've discovered just how many friends we have. Turns out, everyone's a fan when your team is winning!

Which brings us to an important question: Are your stakeholders winning?

Whether you're a franchisor or franchisee, we assume that your product or service is something that customers are willing to pay for. That being said, a business can never get complacent. To succeed in the long term — to be a *Fanchise* — you have to be relentless in improving your product, services and operations.

As we learned over the years, this doesn't always happen in franchising. Case in point: We hired Jim Goniea as our Self Esteem Brands general counsel in 2018. Jim brought two decades of experience working with multiple franchise networks, and he had spent most of his time supporting franchisors. After 18 months on our executive team, he made a surprising observation after a meeting.

"Guys, I've been in franchising almost my entire career, and I've never been with a company that cares so much about franchisee success," he said. "We spend most of our time in these meetings talking about how to make other people money, and we should be proud of that."

"Isn't that normal for a franchisor?" Chuck asked him. "Don't they all focus on franchisee performance, especially when a percentage royalty aligns everyone to success?"

"Unfortunately, no," he said. "I know lots of franchisors who are mostly focused on selling new territories or looking for ways to boost their own bottom lines. I'm not saying that's bad, I'm just saying

I've never been with a company that cares so much about their franchisees."

It's true. Our entire management team is absolutely obsessed with franchisee performance and sentiment. What surprises people even more is that we operate that way even though our franchisor royalties are flat, not based on a percentage of franchisee sales. Conventional wisdom holds that a flat-fee franchisor would be less motivated to obsess about franchisee profits. In our case, the opposite is true.

Maybe that's because we've been entrepreneurs since the age of 20. We ran small businesses for the better part of two decades, so we know what it's like to never feel like you have enough time, capital or resources to compete — let alone reinvest in your business. We feel a massive responsibility to serve every franchisee who puts their hard-earned money into one of our brands. If they show the courage to invest in themselves and us, then we're not going to let them down.

> **Our franchisor royalties are flat, not based on a percentage of franchisee sales. Conventional wisdom holds that a flat-fee franchisor would be less motivated to obsess about franchisee profits. In our case, the opposite is true.**

We always said that no matter how big our company got (and it's gotten quite big), we'd never forget where we started, and we'd always have the souls of small-business owners. During the hiring process, we'd ask a candidate if they had any small-business experience. Maybe they owned one. Maybe a parent or relative had one. Maybe they worked in one as a kid or earlier in their career. Whatever their level of exposure, we could usually trust that if they had experienced the toil and risk of running a business firsthand, they would show authentic empathy and respect for our franchisees.

Hiring people with small-business experience gave us a huge advantage, because franchising too often has an "us vs. them" mentality between franchisees and the franchisor, where head offices are filled with people who have no idea what it takes to run a business.

Does a franchise business have an advantage because the owner can tap more resources and save more time and money in some areas than a traditional business can? Yes, but a franchise investment still requires risk, courage and tons of hard work. *That* should always be respected.

"

We feel a massive responsibility to serve every franchisee who puts their hard-earned money into one of our brands. If they show the courage to invest in themselves and us, then we're not going to let them down.

"

We vowed that in our culture, we wouldn't tolerate any team member who didn't show empathy and respect for franchise owners, period. This mindset showed up in our game plan for winning, which we'll share now.

OUR FOUR STRATEGIC PILLARS: THE GAME PLAN FOR MAKING SURE STAKEHOLDERS WIN

Our overall game plan was driven by an intense focus on four strategic pillars:

#1. Franchisee Revenue & Profitability

#2. Franchise Development: Selling & Opening New Units

#3. Innovation & Differentiation

#4. Operational Excellence

Our tactics would evolve each year, but these fundamental pillars never changed.

Pillar #1: Franchisee Revenue & Profitability

You're likely familiar with terms like "Average Unit Volume" (AUV), "Unit Level Economics" (ULE) and "Same Store Sales" (SSS). These metrics are common across the banking and franchising communities.

Our most important pillar at Anytime Fitness was focused on improving our franchisees' top line, bottom line and performance. That translated to capturing more leads, converting them to memberships, and inspiring our members to improve their health. In turn, that led to people keeping their memberships and referring us to their friends and family.

Franchise
Revenue &
Profitability

This pillar is the fastest accelerant in the *Fanchise* flywheel. When franchisees win, they open more units, provide a reference for new franchisees, and speed up overall brand growth.

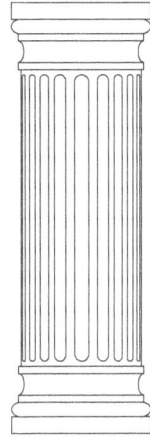

Pillar #2: Franchise Development: Selling & Opening New Units

New territory sales and openings, done sustainably, deliver revenue for the franchisor while also benefiting existing franchisees. More units means a bigger pool of marketing dollars. More marketing dollars means more consumer brand awareness. More brand awareness means more brand loyalty and lower costs to acquire and convert leads into customers. More franchisees also means a larger community of like-minded owners who can support each other while building long-term success.

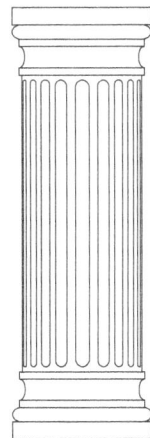

Franchise
Development

101

Pillar #3: Innovation & Differentiation

This pillar focuses on making investments and building capabilities that will deliver competitive advantages long into the future. (It's also a way to budget for skunkworks-type[18] projects that may not always work out.)

We focused on simplifying operations to make it easier and/or less expensive to operate a club; creating better, faster and more personalized ways to support our members; and investing in partnerships to benefit both members and franchisees.

Innovation & Differentiation

One example was our partnership with Apple Fitness+, which provides world-class content that members can access anytime, anywhere. Reducing friction in the member experience required a tech collaboration with the team from Apple, as well as A/B testing with users. The payoff: Our franchisees now have an unmatched value proposition to offer their members, and those members have access to holistic wellness services inside or outside the club.

---

[18] A highly autonomous, confidential and innovative project developed by a small team that's often outside the normal bureaucratic structure of an organization.

Pillar #4: Operational Excellence

Focused on our corporate team, this pillar measured our financial performance, workplace culture and capital investments. We would forecast, budget and monitor top-line growth, expenses, investments, EBITDA margin and employee sentiment. The result: We won numerous awards for being the "Best Place to Work in Minnesota."

Why did we do this? To lead by example, we knew we had to exhibit a winning, high-performance culture that challenged employees while also inspiring them to love their purpose-driven work. That love would then find its way into franchisees and members around the world, continually laying the groundwork for expanding a global *Fanchise*.

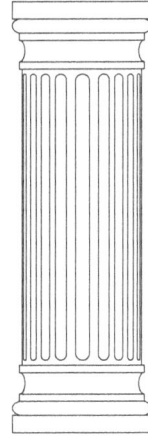

Operational
Excellence

We obsessed over these pillars and never had a shortage of ideas around them, but prioritizing strategies and tactics remained a challenge. Sometimes during healthy debates among leaders, Chuck would ask our team, "If a franchisee was sitting next to you right now, which option would they choose and why?"

Chuck borrowed this approach from Jeff Bezos, who famously kept an empty chair in strategic meetings to represent the Amazon customer. It helped us consider how stakeholders would feel about the decisions we made that day, as well as how they would benefit. It improved our ability to solicit ideas and feedback from customers and franchisees. And it helped us use our Franchise Advisory Council (FAC) to prioritize and make investments on behalf of the entire network.

Business is the ultimate team sport. That's why we routinely told people to disregard titles and tenures in company meetings. Whether you'd been with us 10 years, 10 months or 10 days, we wanted your input.

We also knew that no team or business can win every game, every season (especially teams from Minnesota). In 24 years with Anytime Fitness, we saw it all: the scrappy start-up years, The Great Recession, a crippling pandemic, huge waves of digital and physical competition, and changing trends in fitness and consumer technology. We navigated it by focusing on one thing: *helping our franchisees win.*

Did we win every month and quarter? No. But we listened. We remained adaptable, nimble and obsessed with helping our small-business owners. And we always allocated a healthy amount of capital each year to improve their capabilities.

They knew this. They appreciated it. And together, we created a winning culture and a winning global team. The result has been priceless: loyal, raving fans who stick together through good times and bad. As they say in sports, the most talented team doesn't always win the championship, but the best locker room usually does.

BUILDING A BETTER CONSUMER BRAND

"

If you had to do it all over again, what
would you do differently? **"**

Did we always balance stakeholder interests perfectly at Anytime Fitness? No. In fact, when we speak at franchising events, we're often asked what we would do differently if we did it all over again. Our answer never fails to surprise people:

"We would have built a stronger consumer brand."

The audience knows that we have thousands of locations around the world, so they look confused. *But you already have an incredible consumer brand!*

True, we built a strong consumer brand in many countries outside the U.S. But we usually graded our top brand value propositions like this:

Employee brand value proposition: A

Franchise brand value proposition: A

Domestic consumer brand value proposition: C+

On our home turf in the U.S., Anytime Fitness could have done a lot better with our consumers/members in the earlier years. We started in 2002, and as we've mentioned, it looked like an easy business to replicate. After enjoying some early growth, the race was on. Who would win market share and emerge as the dominant brand? Who could scale quickly and get a foothold in new markets?

We were maniacal in our competitive focus, and we instructed our team to value speed over execution, which led to us selling franchises to anyone who could write a check, regardless of their prior experience or operating acumen.

We also failed to strictly enforce brand standards. And with hyper-fast growth, we didn't have

You get a franchise! And you get a franchise!

the field operations or compliance resources to make every location represent the best look and feel of an Anytime Fitness club. This led to wild inconsistencies in the brand. Visit our clubs in, say, Southeast Asia, and you'll see remarkable consistency. But in the U.S., you can still visit two different Anytime Fitness locations and have two very different experiences. One might be the cleanest, friendliest and best-equipped club you've ever seen. The other won't. If you ran a McDonald's or Starbucks like that, you'd be out of business.

If we could go back in time, we would have built and communicated a consistent story around the brand from day one, and we would have standardized everything early — the member experience, the operations, the marketing, everything.

Anytime Fitness and its franchisees do a much better job today at enforcing brand standards and uniformity. But looking back, we could have walked and chewed gum at the same time in the earlier days. We could have won the market share race while *also* building a trusted brand where members received a consistently memorable experience at each and every club.

Whether you're building a *Fanchise* from scratch or transforming into one, learn from our mistakes: Envision the ideal experience you want your stakeholders — especially your customers — to have, and keep it consistent. As we've learned, that's easier said than done.

FANCHISE "QUESTION & ACTION" ITEMS

For Franchisees

Question: Are you making your customers your biggest fans?

> **Action:** Identify one way this month to surprise or delight your top customers. Make it something they'll want to tell others.

Question: Are your employees motivated to treat the business like it's their own?

> **Action:** Ask your team what rewards, recognition or perks would make their work more meaningful.

Question: Do you treat your franchisor as a true partner, not just a rule-maker?

> **Action:** Reach out to share one success story and one request for support this quarter.

For Franchisors

Question: Do you understand what success looks like for each stakeholder group?

Action: Survey franchisees, customers and employees to learn their top priorities, then act on what you hear.

Question: Are your incentive structures actually driving the behaviors you want?

Action: Audit current rewards, bonuses and recognition programs to ensure they align with your brand mission.

Question: Are you creating a culture of mutual wins?

Action: Share stories of "triple wins" (a decision that benefited franchisees, customers and the brand) and encourage others to do the same.

[7]

FANCHISE YOUR FRANCHISEE/FRANCHISOR RELATIONSHIP

ANYTIME FITNESS ONCE had a franchisee we'll call Scott, who operated a club in a small town in Minnesota for nearly 20 years. Scott was successful, but he had his own ideas about how best to operate and market, and he was never shy about expressing to Stacy Anderson his dislike of the national promotions.

Stacy never gave up on listening to Scott and trying to engage him in the "why" of our marketing and advertising decisions, but nothing seemed to work. It got so bad that Scott eventually refused to speak with or even make eye contact with Stacy at our conferences.

Then something changed.

Covid-19 hit our system hard in 2020 (more on that later), and suddenly Scott was reaching out to Stacy, asking for help and offering up his own ideas. As Stacy and Scott worked together to navigate the unprecedented challenges of mandatory gym closings and a host of new safety regulations, his past rancor melted away.

But that's just the middle of the story.

Tragically, Scott died in 2023. It hit everyone hard, including Stacy. After some time had passed, Stacy ran into Scott's wife, Elise, at a company training event. They talked about Scott's passing and Elise's desire to start over, maybe in France. After all, she had studied in Paris, spoke fluent French and had already attended a fitness conference in the country.

Coincidentally, over the next few weeks, Anytime Fitness was in discussions with a new master franchisee about developing France as a new market. When Stacy heard that we signed a master in France, she remembered her conversation with Elise and emailed her: "Our new master franchisee in France could use some help. Would you like to work with him in Lyon?"

"Honestly, the timing couldn't be better," Elise replied. "I'm ready for a new start! On a personal note, I feel that the timing of your email was a sign. It was on the one-year anniversary of Scott's death. Grief never goes away, but this is the right time to make decisions about the future."

That call was the beginning of a new start for Elise. She currently handles all new franchisee training for our French master with immense gratitude for the email that changed her life at an especially difficult time.

We share this story because it reinforces something we've always believed about franchising: The heart of a *Fanchise* is a healthy, caring franchisor–franchisee dynamic.[19] Beneath all the contracts, royalty payments and occasional disagreements is a human relationship that can be transformative when managed with care and empathy. Even the most challenging franchisee relationships can evolve over time, and the connections we build with each other can transcend business to become deeply personal.

We've seen time and again that Anytime Fitness's strongest competitive advantage isn't our business model or even our brand. It's the authentic relationships we cultivate with our franchisees and their families, especially during life's most challenging moments.

The heart of a Fanchise is a healthy, caring franchisor–franchisee dynamic. Beneath all the contracts, royalty payments and occasional disagreements is a human relationship that can be transformative when managed with care and empathy.

---

[19] Note: When we talk about Anytime Fitness franchisees, we're generally talking about owner/operators who invest with the intention of working in the business and frequently interacting with customers, employees and their communities. We're not talking about the high-net-worth individuals and private-equity funds ("investor franchisees") that typically invest in sectors like quick-service restaurants, hotels, automobiles, pet services and beauty franchises.

WHAT TO LOOK FOR IN A FRANCHISOR OR FRANCHISEE

This is the million-dollar question, and with more franchise businesses emerging than ever before — and more infrastructure and money around promoting them — it's a hard one to answer.

Based on our experience, here's how we would summarize the traits that franchisees and franchisors need to look for if they want any hope of becoming a *Fanchise*.

WHAT FRANCHISEES SHOULD LOOK FOR IN A FRANCHISOR

- They open the door to a community of like-minded entrepreneurs.
- They have a strong brand reputation at the consumer level.
- They truly have a proven product or service with multiple profitable locations.
- They're involved and invested not just in their business but also in their industry.
- They have high standards for new and existing franchisees.
- They exude a culture based on positivity, not fear.
- Their values match yours.
- They're about smart growth, not growth for growth's sake.
- They're fueled by a motivating purpose that goes beyond their product.
- They care about profitability at the individual-unit level.
- They provide strong marketing, compliance and operational support, especially when it comes to technology.
- Their leadership is focused on long-term profitability.

- They have a track record of innovation and constantly improving their core product or service.

- They offer a reasonable exit strategy if the partnership doesn't work out.

WHAT FRANCHISORS SHOULD LOOK FOR IN A POTENTIAL FRANCHISEE

- They believe not only in your product but also in your larger mission, vision and values.

- They understand that a successful franchise takes time, and they're in it for the long term.

- They have a strong work ethic and know they're going to have to put in some long hours.

- They get customer service and that everyone is basically in the service business.

- They know that they need to follow the proven process, but they'll also look for ways to innovate and improve it.

- They'll be willing to share successful innovations to help the entire system.

- They'll always remain curious and eager to learn — both from corporate and from their fellow franchisees.

- They'll always try to solve problems before pointing fingers.

- They're coachable.

- They have basic business acumen and thrive on data.

- They have people skills.

- They have local knowledge and are eager to get involved in their local community.

TOP 5 CHALLENGES IN THE FRANCHISEE–FRANCHISOR RELATIONSHIP & HOW TO MEET THEM

The "zee-zor" partnership can create massive amounts of joy and equally massive amounts of stress. With the assistance of our Expert Panel, we've identified five critical challenges that can make or break a franchise system — and how to address them like a *Fanchise*.

Challenge #1: Setting the Right Expectations

The most pervasive issue in franchising begins before a franchisee even signs on the dotted line: expectations that don't match reality.

"Too many emerging and new franchisors say, 'It's plug and play. Just follow the system,'" says Brian Schnell. "Then when the franchisee has two people not show up to work, instead of saying, 'This is my business; I need to figure it out,' they ask the franchisor how they're going to solve it for them."

This disconnect leads to disappointment and blame, often made worse by brokers and consultants who paint an overly rosy picture of franchising so they can make the sale.

How to Meet It

For franchisees, do thorough due diligence before signing. Talk to multiple existing franchisees — not just the ones the franchisor recommends — and ask tough questions about their day-to-day reality.

As a franchisor, be candid about challenges from the start. For example, most franchisors spend too much time selling "blue sky" when they should be more candid and realistic (see Challenge #2). We tell franchisees, "Frankly, you may love us today, but one day you won't." You have to prepare the new franchisee for down times. That way, when they happen, you can say, "Remember, we talked about this."

Challenge #2: Making "Discovery Days" More Effective

The sales process for a prospective franchisee typically lasts 8–12 weeks, and just about every franchise brand hosts a day at its head office to vet potential franchisees. Some people call it "Signing Day" or "Celebration Day." We call it "Discovery Day."

During this event, the prospective franchisee meets various team members and learns about support capabilities. The franchisor also assesses whether the franchisee has the potential to become a successful operator. Most franchise systems roll out the red carpet and paint a story of wealth and easy times ahead ("blue sky").

We don't, because we believe in candor and large doses of reality.

We talk about the "f" word ("failure"), the hard times ahead, the sleepless nights and the gravity of owning your own business. We tell prospective franchisees that owning a store is like putting on a 40-pound weighted vest that never comes off. We tell them that even under the best leadership, they'll be disappointed by employees who leave at the worst times. And we talk about mistakes we've made as a franchisor. These moments of raw truth build pillars of credibility, accountability and trust.

In a nutshell, a Discovery Day should be about finding the right partners, and it should be a mutual evaluation period. Not every potential franchisee is a good fit for every franchisor, and vice versa. Unfortunately, many Discovery Days become a franchisor sales pitch that makes all parties say "yes" when many should be saying "no."

This matchmaking process requires certain commitments on both sides (see our "Vows" later in this chapter). If you're a franchisor, will you walk the walk when it comes to supporting your franchisees? Will you take a long-term view on success? If you're a potential franchisee, are you truly passionate about the franchisor's brand and product? Are you willing to follow the playbook and burn the midnight oil until the profits roll in?

> **"**
>
> **Not every potential franchisee is a good fit for every franchisor, and vice versa. Unfortunately, many Discovery Days become a franchisor sales pitch that makes all parties say 'yes' when many should be saying 'no.'**
>
> **"**

These commitments are even more important when identifying master franchisees in an international franchise system. Anytime Fitness says no to a higher percentage of masters than domestic franchisees because repping your brand in another country is even more important than owning a domestic storefront (more on this in Chapter 12: "Found in Translation: Taking Your *Fanchise* Global").

How to Meet It

A *Fanchisor* makes Discovery Day an introduction to the organization — not just the building — and inspires potential franchisees to self-select.

During our Discovery Days, we ask questions about our prospects' background and why they're considering our brand. We also love to observe their emotional intelligence in a group setting. Do they practice good nonverbal communication with eye contact and high engagement? Do they show respect for other prospective franchisees' questions? Do they show up with humility, passion and curiosity?

When we've turned down prospective franchisees, the main culprit has usually been arrogance. If someone comes off as uncoachable — like they think they know more than anyone else — then we know they're not going to be a team player. That's important because *Fanchise* relationships are strongest in the most challenging times.

Challenge #3: Not Relying on the Franchise Agreement to Manage the Relationship

Franchisors and franchisees have to have two things: They both need to be profitable, and they have to have codependency. Franchisors are dependent on franchisees, whether they realize it or not. And franchisees need to be dependent on the franchisor.

— Chuck Modell

Many franchisees and franchisors make the mistake of relying on the franchise agreement to guide their working relationship.

"The franchise agreement is there to allow the franchisor to protect the brand, evolve it, change the system, and establish rules and responsibilities, period," says Brian Schnell. "If you're relying on it to govern the actual relationship, then you're in big trouble."

119

"About 50% of all lawsuits that get filed in franchising would be avoided if the franchisor would sit down and have a meaningful business conversation with the franchisee," says Ron Gardner. "Just explain what you're trying to do, why you're trying to do it, and why it's good for the franchisee."

In a *Fanchise*, the franchisee–franchisor relationship happens at multiple levels, from internal forums to your Franchise Advisory Council to your annual conferences. The tools you have depend on your size and scale, but the point is that the relationship needs to be open, honest and (preferably) face-to-face.

How to Meet It

Build real relationships based on trust and mutual respect. Understand that legal documents are necessary but not sufficient. Create open channels of communication and forums for franchisees to voice concerns.

Challenge #4: Involving Franchisees in Decisions and Communicating the "Why"

We teased this story earlier. Here's the full version.

It's 2009, and we're at our annual conference in Atlanta. We're still operating like a start-up, and we're launching a new digital product called Anytime Health that's basically our first attempt to help members improve their health and wellness outside the club.

This launch has financial implications for our franchisees, and it goes over like a dad joke at a funeral. We meet with our Franchise Advisory Council afterward, and they basically say, "What the hell? You never consulted us on this!"

They're right. We pause the program, relaunch it nine months later after incorporating their feedback, and it goes much smoother.

The lesson: We couldn't run our franchise like a start-up anymore. We needed to engage our franchisees more. Ideas could no longer be ours; they had to be *theirs*. This is one of the differences between a founder and a leader: A leader accepts that not every great idea is going to come from them.

In fact, as your system grows, the 80/20 rule will take hold: Most of your best ideas (80%) will come from your customer, or from your franchisees and their staff. Only 20% will come from you. But to get to that 80%, you have to listen closely and sift through the commentary to find the most constructive ideas.

Today Anytime Fitness taps domestic franchisees, members/customers, international master franchisees, and even vendors and suppliers to come up with the next Big Idea. And when we're talking to our brand presidents about a new strategy, we ask, "Would our franchisees like that strategy? Would they agree with it or not?" Our leaders are remarkably transparent, and our franchisee sentiment is as high as it's ever been.

> **This is one of the differences between a founder and a leader: A leader accepts that not every great idea is going to come from them.**

The need to communicate the "why" came up over and over again with our Expert Panel: When franchisors make unilateral decisions

without sharing their thinking, they alienate their franchisees —
especially the ones who've invested their life savings in the brand.

"If franchisors would communicate the 'why' before sending out
emails that say things like 'your tech fees are going up $50 a month,
and don't complain about it because we're not going to talk to you,'
then a whole bunch of franchise lawyers would be out of business,"
says Ron Gardner.

"Too many franchisors and franchisees don't understand that
their success is inherently tied to one another," says Matt Haller.
"From where I sit, a lot of the governmental rules and regulations we
don't like come from a fundamental misunderstanding of the fact
that as a franchisee, you fly the flag of the brand, but you don't *own*
the brand."

How to Meet It

If you're a franchisor, you always need to communicate the 'why'
before major decisions like fee changes and required renovations
(whether in person at an annual conference or via email). In addition,
create a robust Franchise Advisory Council (FAC) that gives your
franchisees genuine input into major decisions.

"I'm just honest with people," says Stacy Anderson, who manages
Anytime Fitness's Franchise Advisory Council. "You have to build
trust, and conflict is connection." (More on how Stacy manages the
Anytime Fitness FAC in Chapter 8.)

Challenge #5. Giving Failing Franchisees a "Soft Landing"

❝

Letting the wrong people hang around is unfair to all the right people, as they inevitably find themselves compensating for the inadequacies of the wrong people.

— Jim Collins, *Good to Great*   **❞**

In franchising, some units will fail. That's just part of the game. When a franchisee needs to exit the brand, a franchisor has the right to pile on more financial obligations. We do our best not to, because maximizing the pain makes about as much sense as keeping a failing operation in business.

Some franchisors, on the other hand, make it nearly impossible for failing units to exit without facing devastating financial consequences. Remember, even landlords have an obligation to mitigate. They have to re-rent the house or apartment. They can't just keep someone on a lease for 15 years. Despite this, the impulse of many non-*Fanchise* franchisors is to "protect the brand" and close the problem unit quickly, with little regard for the franchisee's financial implications.

"If franchisors would find a way to let failing franchisees exit gracefully, we'd have far fewer disputes," says Ron Gardner. "Some franchisors have this idea that 'if you leave, we're coming after you for every penny you would ever owe us.' When you do that, you leave people with no choices. That is one of franchising's most obvious black marks."

123

Remember: When a store or unit isn't performing well, it's not always about the product or competition. Sometimes life gets in the way — serious illness, relocation, divorce, death or natural disasters. When an owner/operator is failing, they're exposed to losing their life savings with future obligations to landlords, lenders, suppliers and the franchisor.

A *Fanchise* thinks differently and creates a "soft landing."

How to Meet It

One day, we learned that one of our club owners had unexpectedly passed away. He owned over half a dozen clubs by himself, with no partner and no family members in the business. His children had no idea what to do.

As a *Fanchisor*, we deployed team members into each club to communicate with employees and members. We helped the children work through legal and financial hurdles. We facilitated a sale of each club, and the children used those proceeds to eliminate their dad's financial obligations with money left over.

We did this because a *Fanchisor* supports its franchisees until the last out. It helps them negotiate with all parties to significantly reduce their liabilities, or it mediates the sale of the underperforming store to a new or existing franchisee.

In most cases, a new owner has a good opportunity to turn a failing business profitable. We've helped it happen literally hundreds of times. Is it easy? No. But it truly protects the brand, saves a store from closing, gives another owner a great opportunity and reduces the exiting owner/operator's obligations. That's the outcome you want.

Building a successful franchisor–franchisee relationship requires work from both sides. You can create a *Fanchise* of passionate brand advocates only when you commit to transparency, communication and mutual respect.

> **A *Fanchisor* supports its franchisees until the last out. It helps them negotiate with all parties to significantly reduce their liabilities, or it mediates the sale of the underperforming store to a new or existing franchisee.**

CAT: COMMUNICATION, ALIGNMENT, TRUST

In *Love Work*, we introduced the concept of CAT as a framework for creating a high-performing workplace culture. We originally applied this concept to our partnership, then to internal team dynamics, but it's arguably most important in the franchisor–franchisee relationship.

After we bought out our third partner in 2009, we brought in a professional psychologist to help move our culture in a more positive direction. This experience taught us that the ultimate success of any relationship depends on talking openly and frequently, reaching agreements on key issues and feeling confident that you can always rely on the other person.

For franchisors and franchisees, CAT is your relationship superpower. It's the foundation upon which a franchise becomes a *Fanchise*.

Communication is about creating a level playing field where every franchisee, whether they own one unit or 50, feels heard. As we mentioned earlier, we routinely tell employees and franchisees to ignore titles and tenures in meetings. We actively seek input from everyone, from brand-new franchisees to veterans. When franchisees speak, we listen before responding.

Alignment isn't about forcing franchisees to think or behave in lockstep; it's about inspiring them to believe in your shared mission. It goes back to communicating the "why." When we introduce a significant change, we provide clarity and focus by explaining the thought and strategy behind every decision. Our franchisees deserve to know what we're doing, why we're doing it and when it will impact their business. They also deserve to know what we're not doing (and why).

Trust requires vulnerability from both sides. When a franchisee operates with good intentions but makes mistakes, we don't overreact with policies that punish the entire system. Trust is both a form of currency and a business multiplier, and it's the natural by-product of strong communication and alignment.

As a franchise system grows, maintaining CAT becomes more challenging, but also more essential for all parties. The bread crumbs of almost every franchisor–franchisee conflict lead back to bad communication, misaligned objectives or lack of trust. As Chuck Modell told us, "When franchisees feel like you care more about opening new units than building on their sales, trust dissipates quickly." When that fundamental relationship breaks down, the only option left is legal battles, which no one wins (except the lawyers).

> **When a franchisee operates with good intentions but makes mistakes, we don't overreact with punitive policies that affect the entire system.**

Remember: The lifeblood of franchising flows through relationships, not contracts.

THE ART OF THE FAC

Ground zero of the franchisor–franchisee partnership is the Franchise Advisory Council. We've seen franchisors hand-select the franchisees on their FACs so they're just "yes men" and "yes women." Bad idea. Franchisors should go out of their way to understand their franchisees' problems and challenges, and they should embrace being challenged themselves.

We've learned that the more transparent we are, the more our franchisees understand how and why we make decisions. That goes both ways, because franchisees need to understand *our* problems as well, and that's harder to accomplish than you think.

We get into detail on this in Chapter 8, and we strongly encourage you to read that chapter. In the meantime, remember: An effective FAC thrives on authentic engagement, meaningful wins and continuous curiosity. Oh, and cocktails don't hurt, either …

YOUR FRANCHISE VOWS

> **"**
>
> **In wrapping up our interview with George Weissman of Philip Morris, I commented, 'When you talk about your time at the company, it's as if you are describing a love affair.' He chuckled and said, 'Yes. Other than my marriage, it was the passionate love affair of my life.'** **"**
>
> — Jim Collins, *Good to Great*

Any business can feel a bit like a marriage, but franchising involves a *series* of marriages. Franchisors and franchisees need to realize that even though each side is going to sacrifice some level of entrepreneurial freedom, they're going to be far better as a team than they could ever be apart.

To achieve *Fanchise* status, we think all franchisors and franchisees should make the following vows to each other.

Franchisor

OUR LADY OF FANCHISING

"In sickness and in health, in profits and in losses, till death do we part."

I, [Franchisor's Name], take you, [Franchisee's Name], to be my legally bound partner in business. From this day forward, I promise to provide you with a proven system, a trusted brand and unwavering support. I vow to uphold the integrity of our brand, to equip you with the tools for success, and to guide you through challenges with patience and dedication.

I pledge to always listen, and to remain transparent in our relationship — offering fair policies, open communication and continuous innovation. Through economic highs and market downturns, I will stand by you, ensuring that we together uphold the standards that make our partnership strong.

I promise to focus not only on your revenue growth and profitability but also on instilling a sense of purpose in everything we do as a team.

I promise not to burden you with unnecessary fees or unrealistic expectations, but to provide a foundation on which you can grow, prosper and flourish.

This is my vow to you, today and always.

129

Franchisee

I, [Franchisee's Name], take you, [Franchisor's Name], to be my trusted guide and business partner. I vow to honor and execute on the systems and values you have built, to uphold the brand with pride, and to operate with integrity and dedication.

I promise to follow the proven path you have laid out while bringing my own passion, commitment and local networks and expertise to our shared mission. I will adhere to the guidelines that ensure our mutual success, while striving to grow our partnership with innovation and hard work.

I vow to pay my royalties with honesty, represent our brand with excellence, and uphold the reputation we build together. Through market shifts and industry changes, I will remain committed, knowing that our success is intertwined.

I will engage and collaborate with other franchise owners to share best practices, learn from each other and look for opportunities to grow the brand within our regions.

With trust, respect and a shared vision,
I enter into this business union with you, today and always.

Together

With these vows, we commit to a partnership built on trust, success and shared ambition. We promise to nurture our business, respect our agreement and work in harmony toward a prosperous future.

May our venture thrive, our brand strengthen
and our relationship stand the test of time.

WHO'S BUSIER?

by Chuck Runyon

I WAS DOING a Q&A session on stage at an Anytime Fitness conference in front of 500 franchisees, club managers and personal trainers when one of the owners stood up and said, "Chuck, you must be so busy, yet when I've personally reached out to you over the years, you've always responded. How do you find the time for your franchisees while also doing all your other work?"

I've been asked this type of question hundreds of times over the years, and the franchisee almost always starts it with "I know you're busy." They assume that running a large franchise with thousands of clubs around the world jams my calendar. That's true to an extent, but my answer that day surprised the audience, and it's a perspective I want every franchisor and franchisee to hear:

"I'm not busier than any of you," I said. "In fact, every single one of you is busier than I am. I have experts and teams of people for every part of my business: finance, marketing, operations, HR, legal, sales, technology. I also have an executive assistant. If any of those leaders left, we'd still have layers of talented people to absorb the work. We also have capital reserves to insulate our company from economic downturns. And if I want to go on vacation for a few weeks, this deep and talented team will carry out the work without skipping a beat.

"Compare that to your daily responsibilities as an Anytime Fitness franchise owner. You don't have the resources to hire all those experts across your business. If one of your key people leaves the business, or a personal situation takes them away for an extended time, you either have to do the work yourself or hire, onboard and train someone to fill their shoes — and that person may or may not turn out to be a good fit. A small business doesn't have large capital reserves, so it's more fragile in turbulent times, and more stressful to own and operate.

"Having a strong franchisor fills in the capability gaps, but there's still not enough time in the day to get everything done. So let me be clear: Your day-to-day job as a franchisee is tougher, more stressful, and more time- and capital-constrained than my job as a CEO."

This perspective means everything in franchising. If you're a franchisor, you have a clear choice to make about your organizational mindset: *Will you be superior or servants to your franchisees?* You can have profound respect and empathy for your franchisees, or you can succumb to self-importance by thinking that your work is more important than theirs.

The latter is an easy trap to fall into, because franchisor CEOs do large-scale strategy sessions where they forecast multimillion-dollar budgets that will touch millions of consumer lives. Over time, organizational self-importance can set in and erode your culture from the top down.

We never had that at Anytime Fitness. In fact, our team sometimes thought Dave and I went too far in the other direction, not showing enough respect and admiration for *them*. I'll admit, we were so paranoid about getting arrogant and complacent that we may have carried it too far at times. But we usually did a good job balancing love, respect and praise throughout the network.

Franchisors: This is one of your hardest tasks. But it's also one of your most important.

Franchisees: Feel free to remind your franchisors of this.

Traditional vs. "Servant" Leadership

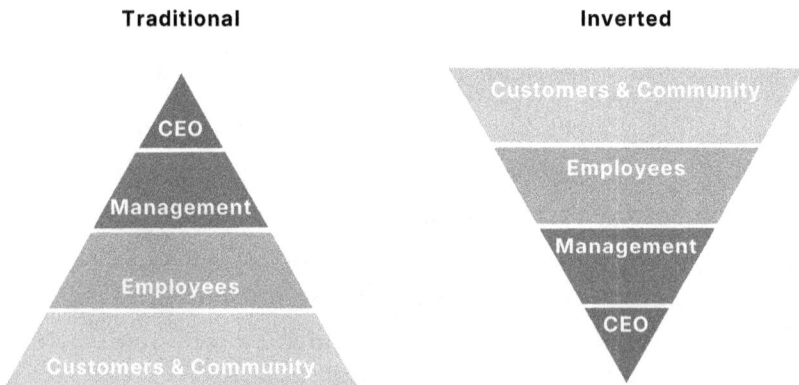

Traditional

CEO

Management

Employees

Customers & Community

Inverted

Customers & Community

Employees

Management

CEO

FANCHISE "QUESTION & ACTION" ITEMS

For Franchisees

Question: Do you understand the "why" behind your franchisor's decisions?

> **Action**: Before reacting to a new policy or program, ask for the reasoning. How does it support the brand and your long-term profitability?

Question: Are you giving feedback in a way that builds trust rather than erodes it?

> **Action**: Ask yourself: *When I disagree, do I approach my franchisor with solutions and openness rather than resistance?*

Question: Are you living up to your side of the partnership vows?

> **Action**: Review this chapter's "Franchise Vows" and identify one that you could improve upon this quarter.

Question: Have you made space for real relationships beyond the contract?

> **Action**: Reach out to your franchisor (or their leadership team) about something other than business. Connection builds trust.

For Franchisors

Question: Are you communicating with transparency, especially about big changes?

> **Action:** Ask yourself: *Do I invite challenge and dissent, or am I surrounding myself with "yes" voices?*

Question: Do you have an exit strategy that allows failing franchisees to leave gracefully?

> **Action:** If not, outline a "soft landing" approach to preserve dignity, relationships and brand reputation.

Question: Are you practicing CAT (Communication, Alignment, Trust) consistently?

> **Action:** Identify one step you can take this month to strengthen each pillar of CAT with your franchisees.

[8]

FANCHISE YOUR FAC

IN 2019, STACY Anderson faced one of the more uncomfortable moments of her career. She was speaking to a group of our U.S. franchisees, talking about the latest changes and additions they needed to make. When her presentation was over, she turned to the group and asked, "Okay, any questions?"

One of our franchisees stood up. "Yeah, I have a question," he said. "When the hell do I start making money with this franchise?"

It was a gut punch. Here was a guy who had invested everything into our brand. Now he was essentially telling our leadership team that we had failed him.

The room went silent. Every eye turned to Stacy. But instead of getting defensive or making excuses, she did what she always does. She looked the franchisee in the eye and said, "You're absolutely right to ask that question. Let's talk about it."

Stacy started a conversation and relationship with that franchisee that deepened for years. She was able to find where we had fallen short. And for his part, he was eventually able to admit that he had made plenty of mistakes that had nothing to do with "Corporate."

None of this took place within Anytime Fitness's Franchise Advisory Council, but we mention it here because it's a great example of how an FAC should work.

If you're a franchisor with an FAC or a franchisee who's part of one, it's critical to understand that these groups don't exist as vehicles for having one-way conversations or to make people feel good about your opinions and decisions. They're ongoing, two-way conversations, and they exist to make decisions that benefit both sides.

No one understands this better than Stacy, who, along with her team, has turned the art of the FAC into a science. Five of the following FAC insights come from her, but we'll start with one of our own.

1. HEY, FOUNDERS, BE STRONG ENOUGH TO ADMIT YOUR MISTAKES!

This goes beyond the FAC, but it's important because success and failure both start at the top.

We're always amazed by how many franchisor founders and CEOs refuse to admit when they've screwed up. Maybe it's ego. Maybe it's fear of litigation. Maybe they think it makes them look weak. Or maybe it's all three. But here's the thing: Your franchisees already know when you've made a mistake. Pretending otherwise doesn't fool anyone. It just erodes trust.

"

[FACs] don't exist as vehicles for having one-way conversations or to make people feel good about your opinions and decisions. They're ongoing, two-way conversations, and they exist to make decisions that benefit both sides. **"**

When we mess up a launch, choose the wrong vendor or make a strategic misstep, we do our best to own it. "We screwed up that execution," we'll tell our franchisees. "The intent was good, but we were wrong."

Vulnerability builds credibility, yet we constantly hear other franchisors say, "Why would we ever admit fault? We'll get sued!" That's exactly the wrong mentality.[20] If you can't be honest about your mistakes, then how can you expect your franchisees to trust you with their livelihoods?

2. STRUCTURE YOUR FAC FOR EFFECTIVENESS, NOT CONVENIENCE.

We typically have 10+ Anytime Fitness representatives at our FAC meetings. And our current FAC has 10 franchisee members in the U.S., representing different regions and types of operators. Eight are elected by franchisees through regional voting because we never want

---

[20] Our attorneys may disagree with us on this.

it to be a hand-picked group of yes-men and -women. We then choose two at-large seats that allow us to maintain diversity of thought and representation from different segments, like multi-club operators or single-unit owners.

FAC members should meet certain standards. They should have a strong understanding of the brand and operations, and they should already have achieved some success within it. If a franchisee is under-performing, then their focus should be 100% on their own business, not the FAC.

3. EMBRACE "PRODUCTIVE CONFLICT."

"The key is cocktails and being nice," says Stacy. But behind the kumbaya, her team has mastered something we call *productive conflict*. "Conflict is connection," she likes to say, and the FAC team walks the walk.

"We like to give the FAC topics that they can wrestle me over," Stacy says. "I might say, 'Let's talk about our priorities this year; what are your top five? Put them on a wall.' If the same issue keeps coming up, and we don't understand why, I'll say, 'Tell us more about why this is so important to you; what are we missing here?' You almost pick the fight. You can do that if you have a base of trust, and doing it reinforces that trust, even if you have to have a hard conversation."

4. BE STRONG ENOUGH TO LOSE.

Some FACs stay in a permanently defensive posture. Franchisors and franchisees see it as a zero-sum game, where the goal is to never give an inch, to double down on every position and to rack up as many wins as possible.

"That's stupid," Stacy says in her characteristically blunt way. "Why can't both sides have wins if it keeps the system improving and moving forward? Our FAC recently covered the details of a club remodel plan. Most of the members objected to a table that they said was expensive and took up too much space. The corporate team wanted to fight them on it. 'Forget it; the table is now optional,' I said. 'Keep it if you want it, get rid of it if you don't.' A table isn't going to change the trajectory of the business."

5. FIND A MEETING RHYTHM THAT WORKS.

Your FAC meeting cadence will depend on the size of your franchise and how geographically spread out you are. The main Anytime Fitness FAC meets quarterly for full strategic sessions, with monthly check-ins on specific initiatives. Stacy's team makes sure that when two members rotate out, two new ones rotate in — never wiping out the entire group at once to avoid a massive learning curve.

The meetings themselves are carefully structured. They start with real business issues, not theoretical discussions. Our team shares actual data and real-world challenges, then asks for franchisees' perspectives on solutions. "We want everyone to participate and be themselves," Stacy says. "If you like to swear, go ahead and swear. I know I do."

When the dust settles, everyone goes to dinner, or Top Golf, or whatever feels right and fun. It's culture-building through hard conversations, followed by relationship-building through shared experiences.

6. DON'T CONFUSE AUTHORITY FOR INFLUENCE.

"Authority is a piss-poor excuse for influence," says Stacy, and she's absolutely right. The moment you start mandating things just because you can, you lose the battle for hearts and minds. The FAC isn't about the franchisor being right. It's about finding the right answers together.

Now, let's be clear: That doesn't mean that a Franchise Advisory Council is a democracy. It's not. But as Ron Gardner says, "The minute I ask a franchisor why they made a particular decision, and they say some version of 'because we can,' my gloves come off."

THE BOTTOM LINE

Fanchises create spaces where stakeholders can bring in competing viewpoints, listen, and modify their plans and ideas based on feedback.

A Franchise Advisory Council should contain a franchise system's most trusted business advisors. These advisors should want you to succeed. They should feel comfortable telling you when you've screwed up. And they should acknowledge when *they* screw up. After all, the alternative is going publicly negative in the press, the courts or social media, and nobody wants that.

When a franchisor fixes their FAC, they can fix their franchise and maybe even build a *Fanchise*. Failure to fix it — or to have one at all — will leave them spinning their wheels and managing conflicts instead of moving forward.

FANCHISE "QUESTION & ACTION" ITEMS

For Franchisees

Question: Are you using your seat at the FAC table, or meetings with your franchisor, to speak with honesty and respect — even when it's uncomfortable?

Action: Before each meeting, prepare one piece of constructive feedback and one solution-oriented idea to bring forward.

Question: Do you approach your franchisor as a partner or an opponent?

Action: Think about the language you use. Replace "you need to" with "how can we" to invite collaboration.

Question: Are you willing to admit when you've made mistakes?

Action: Share openly when your own missteps have shaped your perspective. It builds trust both ways.

For Franchisors

Question: Are you willing to admit fault when you miss the mark?

Action: Model vulnerability by owning one past misstep in the next FAC meeting and sharing how you'll correct it.

Question: Is your FAC structured for diversity of thought, not just convenience?

Action: Audit your current mix of elected vs. appointed members to ensure true representation across your system.

Question: Do you invite and spark productive conflict?

Action: At the next meeting, choose one high-impact topic where you know perspectives differ, and explore it more deeply.

Question: Do you prioritize influence over authority?

Action: Before making a decision, ask yourself: *Am I doing this because it's right for the system, or just because I can?*

[9]

USE PRIVATE EQUITY TO *FANCHISE*

THE INFUSION OF private equity (PE) funds into franchising is one of the most important developments of the last 20 years. It's an incredible resource for both franchisees and franchisors who want to achieve *Fanchise* status, but — and this is a big "but" — it only helps you *Fanchise* if your PE investors are a core value fit with your business.

When we decided to seek a PE partner in 2013, we knew two things: 1) The move was necessary for us and our franchisees to keep growing and evolving; and 2) any PE investor we partnered with had to understand, embrace, and share our culture and values.

For that reason, we took the somewhat unusual step of writing a "manifesto" for interested PE suitors. "This is who we are and what we believe in," it said in a nutshell. "Write us your own manifesto in response. If we think you 'get it,' let's talk. If we don't, we're not interested."

The following are excerpts from that document (except for the cartoon, which we added for fun). We include them here because in many ways, this creates a *Fanchise Manifesto*. Incidentally, the best response we received was from Roark Capital, and they've proven to be a fantastic partner ever since.

THE ANYTIME FITNESS
PRIVATE EQUITY MANIFESTO
(2013)

So you want to invest in Anytime Fitness? First off, we are flattered and humbled because we don't take the responsibility of anyone's investment lightly — including franchisees, vendor partners and investors.

But before we move forward, consider this document a brief summary of our values, our philosophy and the way we view the world, both personally and professionally. If you like what you read, let's continue to explore a partnership to benefit all the various parties involved. If you don't like what you read below, that's perfectly fine. It doesn't say anything bad about you or us; it just means we don't have the required chemistry to go forward, and we can save each other time, money and focus.

ROEI

In the business world, most opportunities are scrutinized through the lens of ROI, and while we understand the importance of that, we prefer a larger meaning in which to operate a business. We use the term ROEI, or Return on Emotional Investment. This is a philosophy that invests and measures success in the areas of People, Purpose, Profits and Play (The 4 Ps).

P #1: People

We're family guys born and raised in Minnesota. Our Midwestern values mean that we aren't flashy or pretentious. We still work our butts off (and love it), but we also find the time to coach our kids' sports teams, and we refuse to miss the important moments of life. Overall, our perspective is that no one wants their tombstone to read "great business person, lousy parent."

These are the most important stakeholders within our system:

1. Employees

We can't expect our franchisees or members to love the AF brand if our employees don't. Everything about the brand starts at HQ, and if we want our clubs to have the best club culture, we need to walk the talk. As the legendary Peter Drucker said, "Culture eats strategy for breakfast."

2. Franchise owners

These are people who've invested their life savings into opening an Anytime Fitness club, and we take that responsibility very seriously. In franchising, the two most important metrics are franchisee profitability and franchisee satisfaction. If you get those two right, future growth will take care of itself.

3. Members (Our Consumers)

The opportunities to meaningfully engage our members will offer brand differentiators to attract and retain consumers in a crowded industry. In addition, our members are an untapped resource to explore loyalty programs or monetization ideas.

4. Vendors

In franchising, vendors and suppliers are expected to provide speedy service, quality products and accessibility to our franchise owners. In return, we provide access to franchisees and important touch points to sell products and services.

5. Investors/Board Members

If we take care of all the stakeholders listed above, the overall performance and investment will take care of itself. We value healthy discussions, new ideas and being questioned on "why" or "how" we do things. We prefer casual board meetings with less reporting and more strategy, a desire for continuous learning and a curiosity about the best business practices from different industries.

P #2: Purpose

The health of this country used to be an asset. Today, it's a liability. Obesity is no longer just a vanity or personal responsibility issue; it's a national economic issue, a societal behavior issue, a generational issue and a national security issue. (From 1998 to 2010, the number of active-duty military personnel considered overweight or obese tripled.)

The declining health of our country concerns and inspires our stakeholders to change lives and bring affordable, accessible and non-intimidating healthy options to their communities. Our owners have seen how physical strength begets emotional strength, which allows someone to overcome depression, eating disorders or taking dozens of medications each day.

P #3: Profits

Franchisee profitability is the most important measurement in every franchise system. Positive cash flow turns big problems into small problems. And profits are the serum for franchisee negativity. Franchisor profitability is also necessary to reinvest into the support needed to grow the network. And with nine college educations to pay for, we need the money!

But in addition to monetary profitability, we offer something that almost no other franchise system offers: a balanced life. The dirty little secret in franchising is that almost every opportunity is advertised as "gain freedom by working for yourself." In reality, most franchisees buy themselves a 50–70 hours/week management role. Thanks to the access system we've created, our owners can leave the club and have time for hobbies, attending kids' events or taking time to enjoy life.

P #4: Play

Aside from alleviating stress and making the workplace more enjoyable, a playful culture stimulates creativity and minimizes the friction that builds between departments in a fast-moving company. And by showing our franchisees the importance of play in the workplace, they can instill this element within their club culture and bring fun, memorable moments to their members.

What are we looking for in potential PE partners?

From our experience in dealing with various partners, some are a bit too obsessed with the financial

ROI. Some of this is understandable because you work in a kingdom where reporting the highest internal rate of return makes you the winner, and it provides a return for your investors along with a gateway to raise more capital and future investments.

But within that context is a potential conflict, because sometimes there's a need to make investments in people, the company, a cause or the system without a direct, measurable ROI.

If we bring on a partner, they must align with the ROEI/4 Ps philosophy with an authentic desire to build a great company that changes lives, makes the world a better place and drives monetary gains. So before we get too far into this process, we'd like to know more about your team.

- Why would you be a strong partner for us? Tell us about your firm and the individuals involved.

- What do you stand for and against?

- What are you like as a person outside of work? What moves you or stirs the passion inside?

- Do you allow your heart and gut to influence a decision as much as your brain?

- Tell us about some of your proudest moments and why. Please share some mistakes or regrets.

- What is the philosophy of your firm? How do you live it or bring it to life? Is it a great place to work? Why?

- Who do you admire and why? Which businesses do you admire?

In closing, we hope you have a better sense of who we are and why/how we operate. We care deeply about the success of this business, and for the monetary and lifestyle ROEI for every stakeholder involved.

People, Purpose, Profits, Play

— Chuck & Dave

PRIVATE-EQUITY PROS & CONS

Our assumption in this book is that whether you're a franchisee or franchisor, you see private-equity money as a growth tool. In other words, if you take it, you plan on staying and continuing to help the business grow. If, on the other hand, you're just looking for a big payday and don't care what happens to the stakeholders you leave behind after the deal is done, then you can skip this chapter (and the rest of the book).

We asked everyone in our Expert Panel to weigh in on private equity in franchising. Rather than trying to summarize what they said, we decided to share their thoughts directly.

Private-Equity Pros

"On balance, private equity has been very good for franchising, especially among the firms whose portfolio companies are in the franchise community."
— MATT HALLER

"Private equity allows people to invest in technology and talent in ways they couldn't do on their own. Overall, that's definitely a good thing."
— JOE FITTANTE

"Private equity has brought more talent into franchising. Twenty years ago, everyone thought PE was going to come in, gut franchisors and squeeze every nickel out of the industry. That hasn't happened because it isn't sustainable."
— BRIAN SCHNELL

"Private-equity finance seems to be pretty good for franchisees, as long as they leave the franchisees alone and help them expand."
— RON GARDNER

Private-Equity Cons

"When private equity comes in that hasn't been involved in franchising, that scares me."
— CHUCK MODELL

"What's negative are those private-equity companies that see franchising only as a great return on investment without appreciating the uniqueness of the franchise or franchisee relationship."
— MATT HALLER

"Good private equity takes a buy-and-hold approach. For too many, it's buy-and-flip."
— BRIAN SCHNELL

"Becoming a *Fanchise* involves heart. And with some PE firms, anything that looks like heart gets yanked out. It looks 'inefficient' to them even though it's absolutely essential."
— STACY ANDERSON

"I talked to someone who used to be on the private-equity side in franchising. I asked her if she was incentivized to help the franchisees, or if it was just about value. She said it was just about value. If franchisees profit, great, but that's not the priority. That concerns me."
— SCOTT GREENBERG

In our experience, PE partners can help you *Fanchise*, but only if they share your values, are in it for the long term and understand what makes your franchise special.

Do PE firms need to make money? Of course they do! "I'm fine when private equity comes in and it's about the money, as long as they understand what's creating that money," says Chuck Modell. "It's not the contracts. It's the culture and the passion."

UNDERSTAND WHAT EACH PARTY BRINGS TO THE TABLE

Especially on the franchisee side, private-equity investments often suffer from a lack of understanding about the partnership.

If you're a mom-and-pop operator with little previous business experience, PE can be a tremendous resource in understanding the business side of franchising. A smart franchisee will take that opportunity to learn the terms, numbers and general financial measurements that PE cares about.

On the flip side, private equity too often undervalues what individual operators bring to the table. PE is so steeped in the numbers that they fail to tap the franchisee's local community knowledge, expertise and reputation — all of which could ultimately add to their profits.

> **If you're a mom-and-pop operator with little previous business experience, PE can be a tremendous resource in understanding the business side of franchising.**

In a *Fanchise* system, each side learns from the other. It's that simple.

DON'T OVERVALUE YOURSELF

Private equity can cause a destructive form of inflation. When PE dollars enter the equation, nearly everyone tends to overvalue their system. Everyone wants top dollar. Everyone sees their upsides. Very few are honest about their downsides.

This is an especially big problem for franchisor founders: They sell too high into a PE deal and stay in the business for a time, then wonder why their PE firm gets pissed off when the business doesn't perform as promised. Dave has literally heard a founder say, "We gave them benchmarks, but we didn't mean we were actually going to hit them!"

IT'S NOT A PAYOUT, IT'S AN INVESTMENT

On both the franchisee and franchisor sides, the biggest mistake both parties make when it comes to private equity is not looking past the transaction. They get their money. They think they deserved it (which they did). But they stop there.

If you're a franchise owner who plans to stick around instead of cashing out, then PE money is an investment, not a prize. What happens after the transaction is more important than the transaction itself.

When we partnered with Roark Capital, we basically saw their investment as a larger-scale version of a franchisee investing in Anytime Fitness. In addition to representing all our franchisee investors, we now represented Roark.

❝

What happens after the PE transaction is more important than the transaction itself.

❞

All of your investors deserve a return, yet too many franchisors and franchisees take private-equity money and don't care about the PE firm's return. After Roark entered the picture, our strong performance set the stage for a long and prosperous partnership. Most recently in 2024, we executed a merger with Orangetheory Fitness (launching Purpose Brands). Again, we showed our new partners our commitment (and competitiveness) through exceptional performance that benefited all stakeholders.

PRESERVING CULTURE POST-PE

> **Founders create a culture, and too many PE firms change it. It's not even intentional. They just don't understand the culture.**
>
> — Chuck Modell

Whether you're a franchisee or franchisor, the introduction of private equity into your business can put your cultural foundations to the test. If they fail, forget about becoming a *Fanchise*.

Disconnects often emerge subtly. Your organizational DNA — the shared values, rituals and communication patterns that make your brand unique — can quietly erode under new ownership that prioritizes standardization and efficiency.

"One of the pitfalls of private equity is that a lot of PE firms say, 'I don't give a damn about your culture,'" says Chuck Modell. "They would open Chick-fil-A on Sundays if they could."

This risk is especially high for franchise systems that have charismatic founders. Passionate franchisee loyalty depends on a cultural alignment that has always come from the top, and now the founders are suddenly out of the picture. As Brian Schnell put it, "When founders exit quickly, franchisees get skittish."

So how do you preserve what matters while embracing necessary change?

Choose the right PE firm. As we noted, we went through rather extraordinary measures before partnering with Roark Capital. (See our criteria for choosing a PE firm next.)

Document your cultural non-negotiables before signing any deal. What traditions, values and relationships define your brand experience? Which organizational behaviors are essential to maintaining franchisee trust?

Secure key cultural ambassadors. These are team members who embody your values and can maintain continuity during transition periods.

Educate your PE partners (assuming they're willing to be educated). The best PE firms understand that the franchise model has always been about relationships.

Measure cultural health with the same rigor you use to track financial metrics. Regular surveys of franchisee satisfaction, employee engagement and customer experience can alert you to cultural erosion before it's irreversible.

Bottom line: Financial engineering may drive short-term growth, but cultural preservation ensures long-term *Fanchise* strength.

TOP 5 CRITERIA A *FANCHISE* USES IN CHOOSING A PE PARTNER

Whether you're a franchisor seeking growth capital or a franchisee looking for expansion funding, choosing the right private-equity partner is critical. Based on our experience and insights from our expert panel, here are the five most important criteria to consider if you want to level up to *Fanchise* status:

1. Franchising Experience & Understanding

Look for PE firms that understand the unique franchisor–franchisee relationship and won't apply generic business strategies that could damage your delicate ecosystem.

2. Time Horizon

Does the PE firm's investment timeline align with your long-term goals? Firms looking for quick exits may push for short-term profits at the expense of sustainable growth. Seek partners whose investment horizons match your development plans.

3. Stakeholder vs. Shareholder Focus

The best PE partners understand that franchise success depends on multiple stakeholders, not just shareholders. They recognize that franchisee profitability, employee engagement and customer satisfaction drive long-term value, not just quarterly returns.

4. Cultural Compatibility

Evaluate whether the PE firm appreciates your culture and values. Request examples of how they've preserved culture in other portfolio companies.

5. Value Beyond Capital

The right PE partner brings more than money. They offer expertise, industry connections, operational improvements and strategic guidance.

Remember: A PE partner can make or break your quest to become a *Fanchise*. The relationship works best when both sides understand that a *Fanchise* is like a stock. It's an investment that requires nurturing, not just harvesting.

FANCHISE "QUESTION & ACTION" ITEMS

For Franchisees

Question: Do you fully understand what private equity means for your business and how it might change your stakeholder relationships?

> **Action**: Evaluate the financial terms, performance expectations and cultural changes that may come with your potential partner.

Question: What capabilities and benefits would you receive with a PE investment?

> **Action**: Write down what success will look like with this new partnership and ensure you have considered potential opportunities and risks.

Question: Are you building reasonable targets that you can actually achieve?

> **Action**: Ask yourself, "Would I bet on me based on the projections I put in place?"

Question: How can you protect your profitability and culture during and after a PE transition?

> **Action**: Build strong relationships and expectations between all shareholders and the franchise network while advocating for employee and customer needs.

For Franchisors

Question: Are you clear on whether private equity is the right move for your brand *now,* or if you're still in the "prove the concept" stage?

Action: Audit your brand's readiness for scale by assessing unit-level profitability, operational support systems and cultural strength before seeking PE partners.

Question: Have you defined your non-negotiables before entering private-equity discussions?

Action: Document your cultural values, franchisee priorities and growth philosophy so you can evaluate PE offers against *them*, not just the dollar amount.

Question: Will this potential PE partner invest in your culture as much as your financial growth?

Action: Use the "4 Ps" (People, Purpose, Profits, Play) as a lens to interview PE candidates and ensure that their vision aligns with your brand's DNA.

[10]

FANCHISE YOUR TEAM

"

Work should be personal — not for just the artist and the entrepreneur. Work should have meaning for the accountant, the construction worker, the technologist, manager, and the clerk. Infusing work with purpose and meaning, however, is a two-way street. Yes, love what you do, but your company should love you back.

— Howard Schultz, *Onward*

"

SOME FOUNDERS AND other franchise leaders push themselves and their teams into burnout. Others demand perfection without looking in the mirror or recognizing that growth only comes from taking bold steps and occasionally falling on your face. Still others think they have to cater to every employee demand and shower them with benefits to boost performance.

If you want to build a *Fanchise*, none of these approaches will work.

Fanchising your employees doesn't mean scolding them or coddling them. It means respecting them, which means being encouraging, empathetic, honest and transparent, and dishing out the occasional dose of tough love. Over the years, we've had our share of occasions to do all of the above, and every time, the feedback from employees has been overwhelmingly positive.

In the spirit of "show, don't tell," here's an example of employee communication that resonated with the right people and moved us closer to *Fanchising* our team. Whether you're a franchisee or franchisor, do you have the internal culture to be able to talk to your team this way? If not, why?

From: Chuck & Dave

To: All Staff

Subject: What Culture Isn't

If an outsider is trying to uncover the foundational elements of what makes our culture remarkable, they'll likely start by studying our DNA, mission and vision statements. And while it's important to write down and establish what our culture is, let's also discuss what remarkable culture isn't.

Remarkable culture isn't about control.

Intelligence, creativity and passion shouldn't be suppressed. Therefore, we grant a tremendous amount of autonomy as team members problem-solve or bring new ideas to market.

Remarkable culture isn't about keeping everyone happy.

Although our employee turnover has been minimal, people have left Self Esteem Brands to pursue new opportunities, and that will happen again during the years ahead. But that's okay, because as life changes, people need to "climb a new mountain."

We've also had to terminate people for a variety of reasons, and often times, the strategic pivoting of a company requires difficult personnel changes. For everyone reading this email, there are varying levels of job satisfaction that fluctuate constantly. Every company, including ours, is not immune to the complex range of human emotions, and we still have plenty of room for improvement.

Remarkable culture isn't cheap.

Per employee, we reinvest more than most companies, and we remain committed to providing opportunities and resources for personal and professional growth.

Remarkable culture isn't infallible.

Every so often, someone takes advantage of our trusting culture. In some companies, the response from senior leadership or HR is to implement new ironclad policies to prevent this behavior and, like a cultural tranquilizer, the fertile soil of a trusting culture is slowly poisoned by the mistrust of a few.

Admittedly, there have been times when we've felt taken for granted, but we won't stop trusting the many over the actions of the few.

Remarkable culture isn't easy.

As we grow, our culture becomes increasingly more fragile, and with off-site team members, the difficulties are magnified. Culture is intangible; it's a feeling that dissipates over time and distance and reminds us of the limitations of "virtual." It's like watching a concert on YouTube versus being in the front row with your friends. You can still enjoy the music and admire the artistry, but you won't feel it pumping through your body. A remarkable culture is a rich, empowering experience, and if it was easy to produce, every company would have it.

Remarkable culture isn't about toga parties.

Great culture has never been built around a partying atmosphere. In fact, we used to have parties more often, and our culture wasn't nearly as strong. Now we party less and work harder, but our culture is better. This indicates that people need to be challenged, to push themselves for growth, accomplishment and purpose.

Remarkable culture is never finished.

This is about all of us. From the outside, people only see meteoric growth without the knowledge of setbacks, problems or the trials and tribulations that accompany a fast-growing franchise amidst an uncertain economic decade. And most of them will never comprehend the tenacity, nimbleness and boundless positive energy needed from a fully engaged team to build a company and remarkable culture that changes lives.

— Chuck & Dave

DESIGNING A *FANCHISE* CULTURE FOR EMPLOYEES & TEAM MEMBERS

The employee aspect of *Fanchising Your Franchise* is so important that we wrote *Love Work* to focus on internal culture and the 4 Ps of People, Purpose, Profits and Play.

People come first in the 4 Ps for a reason. As one of our team members recently told us, "Anytime Fitness employees are your biggest fans because you always cared about them as humans. You took the time to get to know them and their families. Even my kids are your fans!"

Since we covered the 4 Ps in the Private Equity Manifesto, here we'll summarize some other key points from *Love Work*. Bottom line: Whether you're a franchisee or franchisor, you can't build a *Fanchise* until you've *Fanchised* your team. That means focusing on five key areas: hiring/recruiting, onboarding, the day-to-day, evaluation and feedback, and investment.

1. HIRING/RECRUITING

Like NFL teams that conduct rigorous player evaluations before investing millions of dollars into them, you have to evaluate people using a high-performance grid. In our case, we used a vertical axis that represented "ability to get shit done" (talent) and a horizontal axis that represented "culture fit."

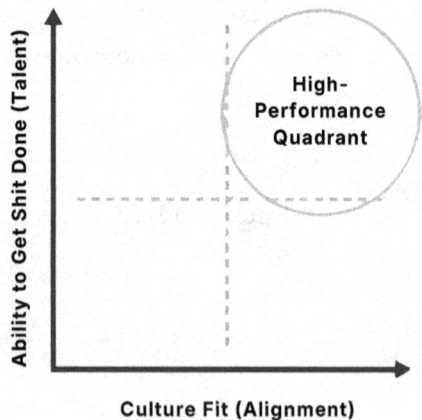

High-Performance Quadrant

Ability to Get Shit Done (Talent)

Culture Fit (Alignment)

Finding people whose values overlap with yours creates collective interest, which is the sweet spot for high engagement. Only *you* can know your specific values, but ours were:

Self-Awareness: People with strong self-awareness have higher emotional intelligence, which leads to better peer interactions.

Sense of Humor: The ability to take work seriously without taking yourself seriously brings Play to the workplace.

Competitiveness: In a brutally competitive business world, we want people who value winning and are bothered by losing.

Passion: That fire you can see in someone's eyes when they talk about something they really care about.

Selflessness: The capacity to help others achieve better health requires natural empathy and a willingness to sacrifice.

Small-Business Experience: No matter how big a franchise system gets, it's still made up a dozens, hundreds or thousands of small businesses. You have to know that world.

Once you create a *Fanchise*, you'll be amazed at what it does for recruiting. Jessica Schneider, the senior director of People Operations at Purpose Brands, recently told Chuck: "I paid my way to Minnesota to interview for Anytime Fitness. When you asked me why, I said, 'Because I love the brand and I didn't want to miss the opportunity.' You paid me back, but it says a lot that I was that much of a fan!"

2. ONBOARDING

After a Halloween party where Chuck couldn't recognize an employee who had already been with us for a month (Chuck thought he was an *actual* UPS delivery man), we developed an onboarding process that included day-one activities (introductions, company history, lunch with team members), and first-week/-month activities (setting goals, scheduling check-ins, training). We also shared photos and bios in the company newsletter. And our most popular and effective tradition was "Rookie Skits," where new hires shed any shyness or self-consciousness and perform a skit for the company.

3. THE DAY-TO-DAY

We covered this in Chapter 7. The foundation of any relationship depends on talking openly, reaching agreement on key issues and feeling confident in mutual reliability. You guessed it, this is CAT: Communication, Alignment and Trust.

4. EVALUATION AND FEEDBACK

Once you establish CAT, evaluation and feedback happen naturally. Our formal review process covered performance, development, key objectives, cultural values, compensation and open Q&A.

5. INVESTMENT

We had a long-standing policy of investing a percentage of our top-line revenues into employee development — not just for job training but also for personal development. Some leaders take an attitude of "why would I invest in people who might take that knowledge and then leave?" Our response (and we're not the first ones to say it): *That's better than not investing in them at all and having them stay!* The personal development side might be even more effective. When someone in IT or accounting can finally take those guitar lessons, they're a fan for life.

COMMUNITY ENGAGEMENT

What makes one franchise operation succeed and another one fail in the exact same area? Lots of factors, but one that has always been clear to us is *community engagement.* Businesses, especially franchises, whose employees get involved in their local communities almost always do better than those that don't. In fact, community engagement is vital to the entire franchise operation.

"The franchisees are closer to their employees and to the local community than the franchisor is," says Matt Haller. "They're giving back to the community in a way that a corporate-run chain can't, because the corporate headquarters simply isn't there."

Anytime Fitness makes a point of recognizing its Community Outreach Club of the Year at every franchisee conference. The most prolific winner of that award — and the poster child of Anytime Fitness's community involvement — is Cleveland-area franchisee Anna Dey. Anna has raised nearly $1 million for charity over the years, embedding her business and team into her local community's fabric like no one else. She also has the most tattooed members of any club in the world (40+). This engagement transforms employees and customers into fans who view the business as essential to their community's identity.

> **Anytime Fitness makes a point of recognizing its Community Outreach Club of the Year at every franchisee conference.**

The payoff isn't just emotional; it's financial. Anna's club achieved Club Platinum status, meaning it sits in the top 5% of the Anytime Fitness franchise system. As we previously mentioned, we see a strong correlation every year between community engagement and profitability. If you want to *Fanchise* your franchise, then you need to become an irreplaceable part of your local ecosystem.

STEAL THESE IDEAS

EVERY COMPANY CULTURE is unique, but here's a list of things we've done at Anytime Fitness to build our *Fanchise* culture.

- **Well-Being Fridays.** Employee engagements consistently show that the number-one thing people look for in an employer is "someone who cares about my overall well-being." That inspired us to give employees Fridays off between Memorial Day and Labor Day. The purpose: Disconnect, be with friends and family, and have "less screen time and more green time."

- **Sharing Private-Equity Proceeds.** When we received a PE payout, we shared a portion of it with our entire team.

- **Annual Traditions.** Like a family, we created annual traditions that meant something. Our Halloween parties became legendary for inspiring staff to connect, compete, laugh, have fun and look forward to the next one.

- **Christmas/Holiday Checks.** We gave employees $100 per year of employment around the holidays.

- **Getting People Involved in Charitable Efforts.** Our HeartFirst Charitable Foundation was funded by participating Anytime Fitness clubs that contributed $100/month to support military veterans through grants and scholarships to help them open their own franchises. Rather than create our own 501(c)(3), we also partnered with Tee It Up for the Troops to help veterans experiencing challenges with emotional detachment and unemployment.

- **Walk-abouts.** We would take any employee for a walk on our HQ's one-mile outdoor trail as an opportunity to get to know them better and answer their questions about the business. Some of our best ideas came from these walks, and they also gave us an accurate snapshot of the health of our internal culture.

- **Departmental Q&As.** We put ourselves in the hot seat and fielded questions from full departments and subsets of teams. They were encouraged to ask anything and force healthy conflict. It wasn't always easy, but these experiences allowed people to feel heard, and they dramatically improved our CAT.

- **Open-Door Policy.** We encouraged anyone in the company to walk into our office and talk to us about anything.

- **Safely Pushing People Outside Their Comfort Zones.** We literally gave someone with a fear of heights the opportunity to overcome it by jumping out of an airplane. She did it, and it changed her life: Addressing her fear of heights helped her overcome her fear of public speaking. (There are other examples, but that's the most dramatic one.)

- **Unlimited PTO.** This sometimes gets a bad rap because it can lead to unclear expectations and people actually being more afraid to take time off. But in our case, it built a deeper level of trust and put the focus on performance, not hours worked.

- **Handwritten Notes.** Never underestimate the power of a good handwritten thank-you, anniversary, random recognition or condolences note. We've written plenty of them, and we're now learning how often people kept them.

- **Jersey Retirements.** In true "fan" fashion, we've brought back team members who left Anytime Fitness to recognize and honor the contributions they made while they were there. Most companies wouldn't think of celebrating their former employees. We put them in our own Hall of Fame.

KENDRA BROOKS

by Chuck Runyon

I FIRST SAW Kendra Brooks at our annual conference in Chicago in 2011. We were both in a long line at the coffee shop, and I spied her from the back. She had no idea who I was, but I felt like I already knew her life story because we had put it together in an Anytime Fitness Member Success Story video that would be shown the next night in front of more than 2,000 people.

To everyone else in line, Kendra was just a normal, beautiful woman waiting to order some coffee. I knew that she had battled bulimia and nearly given up on everything until a personal trainer at one of our gyms took her under her wing and completely changed her life.

That night, a good chunk of our employees and franchisees saw the video on Kendra and quickly found the Kleenex as she took the stage to accept her award. She thanked us and her trainer, and then her husband stepped up to the mic and said, "Thank you for giving me my wife back. Without all of you, she wouldn't be here today."

This was the very essence of a *Fanchise* moment. Through their collective passion and purpose, every person in that room was responsible for saving the life of one of our members.

I went back to our team and said, "Look, everyone in your life might be going through something. A friend, a family member, a stranger at the grocery store, you name it. It's our job to lean in, be empathetic and be that special person who's willing to listen."

I knew from experience that creating the impact on that one person shown in that one video starts with our team. And that's where becoming a *Fanchise* starts too.

FANCHISE "QUESTION & ACTION" ITEMS

For Franchisees

Question: Are you hiring for skill alone, or for skill *and* shared values?

Action: Identify your top five non-negotiable cultural values and ensure every interview question ties back to them.

Question: Have you truly *onboarded* your people, or just handed them a handbook?

Action: Map a first-week experience that makes new hires feel connected, seen and excited to contribute.

Question: Do you know your employees' personal goals, as well as their performance goals?

Action: Ask each team member what they want for their own life in the next year and find one way to support it.

Question: How are you embedding your business in the community?

Action: Choose one cause, event or organization this quarter that your team can rally around together.

For Franchisors

Question: Does your culture travel well?

Action: Evaluate whether the values and behaviors that work at HQ are showing up in every franchise location. If not, why?

Question: Are you investing in your people's growth beyond their job description?

Action: Budget a percentage of revenue for professional and personal development, then communicate that investment clearly.

Question: Do your teams feel trusted or managed?

Action: Audit your policies for signs of over-control that stifle creativity. Replace one with a trust-based approach and track results.

Question: Are you living your values in how you treat employees, customers and partners?

Action: Pick one daily action that visibly reinforces your values to your team and members.

STRESS-TESTING YOUR *FANCHISE*: LESSONS FROM A CRISIS

❝

In my area, so many other clubs and studios closed for good, and without being a part of Anytime Fitness, I also would have closed. I've never been more thankful to be part of this franchise. **❞**

— An Anytime Fitness Franchisee to Chuck

"THAT WAS COLDER than a kiss from my mother-in-law!" laughed Tony Mitchell, our VP of International Development. We were sitting in white terry cloth robes with Tony and Eric Keller, our first Anytime Fitness franchisee, in the parlor of a 210-foot ship docked in Antarctica. As we sipped coffee and Baileys after polar-plunging into the icy Antarctic waters, we all felt like we were on top of the world. We were actually at the bottom of it.

It was day 5 of an epic, weeklong trip of snowshoeing, whale watching, kayaking around icebergs and, most importantly, working out in the Anytime Fitness club on the ship. And we were feeling good as we celebrated the fact that we were now the only fitness and franchise brand on all seven continents.

It was December 2019.

Chuck had also recently invested in a wellness retreat complex across the lake from his family cabin so we could host leadership and wellness retreats for franchisees and members. And we had just conducted our last board meeting of the year with Roark Capital, our private-equity minority partner, where we shared the exciting news that 2020 was set to be our best year ever — with hundreds of new franchises sold, hundreds more opened, new countries penetrated, and double-digit increases in membership growth and key financials.

What could possibly go wrong?

At no point during the board meeting, during our time in Antarctica or while Chuck signed the papers on his new lakefront property did one of us stop and say, "Hey, just spitballin' here, but hypothetically — I mean just for shits and giggles — what would happen if we had to suddenly shut down our entire global network of 3,500 clubs?"

To make what was about to happen even more dramatic, by early March 2020, our rosy financial forecasts were playing out. We were on pace for the best single quarter of performance in our 18-year history, setting us up for our best year ever.

Were we aware that a mysterious virus was impacting certain regions across the ocean? Of course. But like so many others, we thought it would be contained. And like so many others, we were wrong.

By March 13, we were seeing the writing on the wall. So we took a deep breath and sent the following message to all Self Esteem Brands staff. Consistent with our approach from the beginning, it was all about caring and empathizing with our franchisees.

From: Chuck & Dave

To: All Staff

Subject: An Unprecedented Crisis

Sherpas:

The world is experiencing an unprecedented crisis, and during times like this, people need us.

- Self Esteem Brands has the capital, resources and revenue diversification to weather this

storm, but most of our franchisees
don't. Therefore, the uncertainty of this
situation is highly stressful for them.

- SEB employees receive a paycheck when the
  business goes down. Some of our franchisees
  may not be in that position.

- You work for an employer with generous
  benefits of health care, sick leave and
  unlimited PTO, yet we have thousands of
  people employed by our franchisees who
  don't.

- More than ever, our franchisees need our
  support. This may be in the form of
  emotional support (longer phone calls) and
  specific coaching with localized tools to
  navigate this rapidly changing situation. They
  need to feel your care, coaching and
  connection.

You now understand the difference between being
employed vs. being self-employed. For that reason, we
must always show respect and admiration for franchise
owners who've consciously accepted the risks of
owning their own business. During times of crisis, we
may need to put people on our backs and carry them
up the mountain.

There is an SEB response team actively monitoring
the situation and anticipating/developing solutions for
every SEB stakeholder.

We're available to anyone, anytime.

— Chuck & Dave

Just three days later, it had become clear that the virus was spreading quickly (along with the panic and chaos). The worst-case scenario was about to happen. That morning, before sunrise, Chuck wrote the following email to our entire team. It would come to be known as "The Rise Email."

From: Chuck Runyon

To: All Staff

Subject: Rise

As I write this email, it's dark outside my kitchen windows. It seems like a typical pre-dawn morning, but it's not. It's unlike any Monday morning in our lifetime, and the weeks ahead are filled with fear and uncertainty as the world operates without a script.

Some of us have experienced similar situations: The dot-com crash of 2000, 9/11, The Great Recession of 2008–2009. Even more worrisome, the impact of Covid-19 has the potential to dwarf those earth-rattling events.

This is a generational moment, one that will alter future behavior, attitudes and cultural norms.

This is a defining professional moment, and more than any time in our 19-year history, every ounce of your talent is needed. Every minute you can spare. Every bit of energy you can muster. Every selfless idea and action.

This is a defining life moment, and when you look back years from now, you'll remember how you responded. How you contributed to solutions. Provided calm leadership and support. Displayed perseverance, adaptability, creativity and optimism.

You're going to get through this.

We're going to get through this.

We have to get others through this.

That's what leaders do, and SEB has always been a company of leaders.

In a few minutes, the sun will fill the sky with light and hope. During the design phase, we wanted the largest portion of our headquarters building to face east to capture the rising optimism of each new day. This represents our mindset, and we've loved Mondays as much as weekends because we're grateful for the opportunity to perform meaningful work with a passionate, talented team. Despite these dizzying times, today is no different.

It's time for all of us to rise.

— Chuck

THE NEXT TWO weeks were a blur as our team spent day and night shutting down clubs across 40 countries and 12 time zones. Our first priority was supporting and communicating to our members by offering digital coaching, support and wellness tools. Our next priority was focusing on our global network of franchisees, most of whom were owner/operators who lived in the communities they served.

Covid was especially hard on small-business owners, because they didn't have the liquidity or cash reserves of a larger company. Worse yet, policymakers and health experts around the world failed to include "fitness" under "essential services," so while restaurants and liquor stores got to stay open, gyms had to shut down.

(We could fill another book with rants about this, but we'll try to stay focused …)

Along with Roark Capital, we partnered with America's Charities to donate $1 million in direct financial assistance to frontline workers, including thousands of franchise employees and corporate studio and club staff across the Self Esteem Brands brand portfolio. Would it be enough?

During the two weeks that we had to shut down our global network of small-business owners, we've never been more proud of our team. The People foundation we had built over the years paid off in spades, as people who shared our values and were committed to a higher purpose offered priceless operational and emotional support to millions of members and thousands of franchisees around the world.

187

After taking care of our members and franchisees, our third priority was focusing on our own company and making some of the most difficult decisions leaders have to make. Needless to say, when your business comes to a screeching halt, so does your revenue. We had stopped charging royalties to franchise owners, and no one was prepared to buy a franchise. We went from our best quarter to suspending all revenue channels, and no one knew what was going to happen next.

As leaders, we had to consider the cash reserves needed for an uncertain future, and that meant facing the prospect of doing something we'd never done before: laying off employees. Yes, after 18 solid years of growth, internal promotions and cultivating a talented team, we had no choice but to let some people go.

We assembled our top leaders and asked them to reduce our workforce by 20% to protect cash reserves for an uncertain future. We agreed to notify people on Friday, March 27, and this is how Chuck remembers that time:

On Thursday evening, the day before our layoffs, I went to the Anytime Fitness gym at our corporate Self Esteem Brands office. I was completely by myself. Covid meant that no one was coming into the office. All of our Anytime Fitness club locations were closed. And after a long day of work, I needed to work off my stress.

Except I wasn't working out very hard. I was going through the motions, feeling the heavy weight of the next day.

Outside of work, our employees had their own Covid issues to deal with. Their kids were home from school. Some couldn't see or care for their elderly parents. Others had spouses whose jobs were also likely to be affected. These were people with mortgages, tuition payments and living expenses, all feeling the stress of an uncertain future.

It's worth remembering that at this point in the pandemic, no one knew how deadly the virus was or how long the shutdown would last. Fear, uncertainty, misinformation and the politicization of Covid had everyone on edge. And now we were going to lay some of our team off, which would make their lives even less certain and more financially fragile.

Could we have kept everyone on the payroll until business resumed? There were stories about some companies doing that, and Dave and I agonized over the idea, but facing an uncertain future, we had to protect the company's capital reserves to survive. "Hope for the best, plan for the worst."

After a frenetic two weeks of intense stress, and on the eve of company layoffs, I stopped my half-assed workout, sat down in the gym and cried. I cried tears for our employees, and I cried tears for our franchise owners around the world. Some people would lose their jobs. Others would lose their clubs.

As a complicated patchwork of hyperlocal policies were announced in the weeks and months that followed, our team worked around the clock and in every time zone to support members and franchise owners. It felt like every city, county, state, province and country was going to have its own set of rules for reopening. We would literally have clubs just a few miles apart with completely different rules.

The silver lining to the crisis was the pride I felt in how our franchisees and employees responded to it. This is when you find out what people are made of, and actions speak louder than words. A few examples:

- Our team got on the phone seven days a week with franchisees, answering questions like "How can I source materials to put partitions between treadmills?"

- We immediately negotiated with landlords and vendors to provide relief for our franchisees.

- We created digital workouts and coaching services for members so they could stay healthy during lockdowns.

- Our tech team wrote a club reservation program so we could limit the number of members at certain times of the day, which allowed several clubs around the world to get back to serving members and earning revenue.

Another silver lining: Covid added a sense of urgency to our meetings that felt more like our start-up days. After the pandemic passed, we would say, "Hey, why were we so decisive, trusting and focused during Covid, and now we're back to this slog?"

In the end, our Fanchise nature — our collective work ethic, passion, collaboration and ingenuity — enabled us to close far fewer clubs than the rest of the industry. We protected the life savings of our franchisees. And we helped everyone bounce back as quickly as possible after Covid.

We all wish the pandemic had never happened, but it did. And as I look back, it was the proudest moment I've ever felt for our teams. In fact, I'm not ashamed to say it, thinking about it as I write this makes me cry all over again ...

This was the hardest and most humbling experience of our leadership tenure. Yet amazingly, we didn't receive a single complaint. In fact, we got letters and calls and had face-to-face moments with exiting team members who said *thank you, we understand, this must have been hard for you* and *good luck*. These same messages came to us from closing clubs, as well as from just about every stakeholder in our system — proof that building a *Fanchise* can make even the hardest moments a little easier.

"VIEW FROM THE PANDEMIC TRENCHES"

by Stacy Anderson

WHEN COVID-19 FORCED gyms to shut down worldwide, our Anytime Fitness team faced an unprecedented test. The pandemic didn't just challenge our business model; it threatened to break bonds that had taken decades to build.

In my mind, there was only one way to go: be human. In those early days of March 2020, we called our franchisees and said, "Look, we're going to be in the ditch with you."

They told us that this challenge was unlike anything they'd ever faced. Forced closures, aging parents, kids suddenly home from school, revenue disappearing overnight. We were providing emotional support as much as business support, and let me tell you, most of the tears shed had nothing to do with business.

What separated us from other franchise systems during the pandemic was how we approached it. Instead of retreating to protect corporate interests, we

192

leaned in and said, "How can we help?" We worked seven days a week, taking calls at all hours, and helping franchisees navigate everything from landlord negotiations and bank payments to sourcing plexiglass partitions and hand sanitizer.

Not to use a sports cliché, but we took things one day at a time. We'd say to our franchisees, "Here's what we're going to do today." The next day, we'd rinse and repeat. "Here's what we're going to do today." The pattern offered a sense of stability when everyone felt overwhelmed by uncertainty.

Our Fanchise approach worked. While 25% of the fitness industry went out of business during the pandemic, we lost only 3% of our clubs globally. By 2021, our franchisees were making 20% MORE than they had in 2019. The fees they'd once questioned — especially for digital tools — seemed brilliant when the pandemic suddenly made them essential.

The true measure of a *Fanchise* is like the true measure of a person. It doesn't happen when times are good. It happens when everything goes to hell. During Covid, we proved that when you build genuine relationships based on trust, those bonds only get stronger under pressure. It reminded us why we chose to join this franchise in the first place. It reminded us that we were a *Fanchise*.

A MOMENT OF GRATITUDE

If you're still wondering why you should bother putting in the time and effort to build a *Fanchise* instead of settling for a franchise, hopefully this chapter has answered your skepticism.

A *Fanchise* isn't a "nice to have"; it's a "need to have." It's like having flood insurance in a hurricane zone. If we hadn't built a system of raving-fan stakeholders around the world — staff, members, franchisees, suppliers and investors — we never would have weathered the Covid storm as well as we did.

The bookend to our *Fanchise* pandemic experience happened at our Dallas conference in November 2021 in front of nearly 3,000 franchisees and other stakeholders gathered in a giant hotel ballroom. As we looked back over the 1.5 years that had passed since we sent the "Rise" email and watched our industry plunge into chaos, we found ourselves at a loss for words.

At one point, we asked everyone from our corporate team to stand up. As we looked out over their faces, our chests tightened, lumps formed in our throats, and it was hard to get the words out. We didn't just see 150 people standing in a huge hotel ballroom. We remembered how tirelessly they had worked over the previous 20 months — through frustrating global shutdowns and reopenings, the murder of George Floyd and the riots that literally burned through our neighborhoods, the thousands of urgent phone calls, the tough decisions, the emergency meetings, the shift to digital solutions.

When we asked the audience to thank our team, they gave an emotional standing ovation. Writing this book is one thing. But if we could make you feel and experience that moment for yourself, you'd know exactly what it's like to have a *Fanchise*, and you'd never settle for anything less.

Thanks to being a *Fanchise*, we realized that by 2023 we hadn't just survived the pandemic, we'd come out of it better than before.

At our conference in Colorado Springs that fall, Stacy Anderson choked up as she shared the stats and graphics:

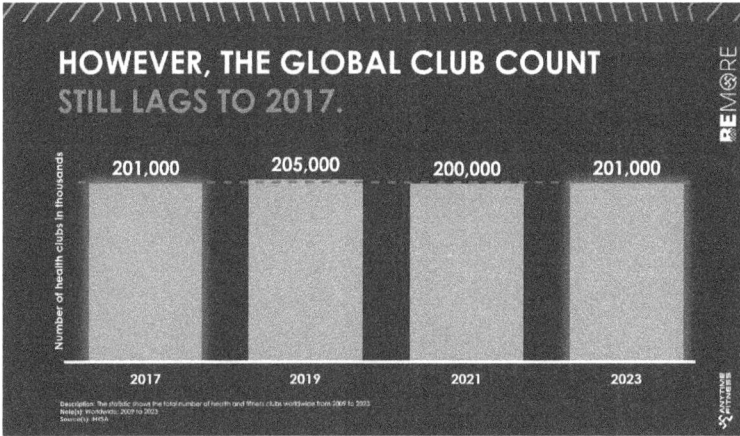

Number of gyms for all fitness franchises globally: stagnant.

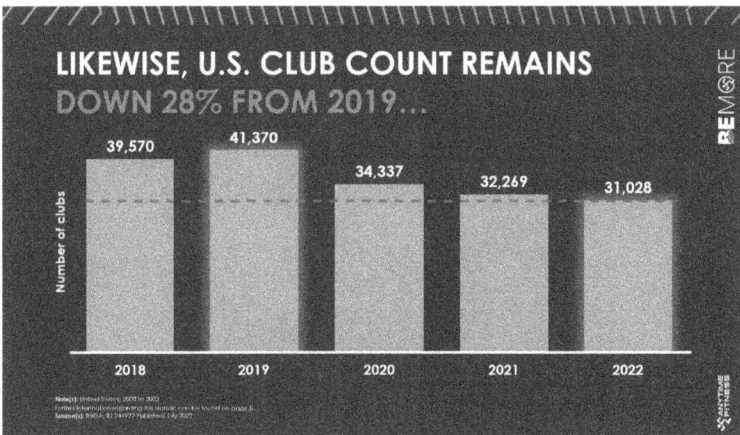

Total number of gyms in the U.S.: down.

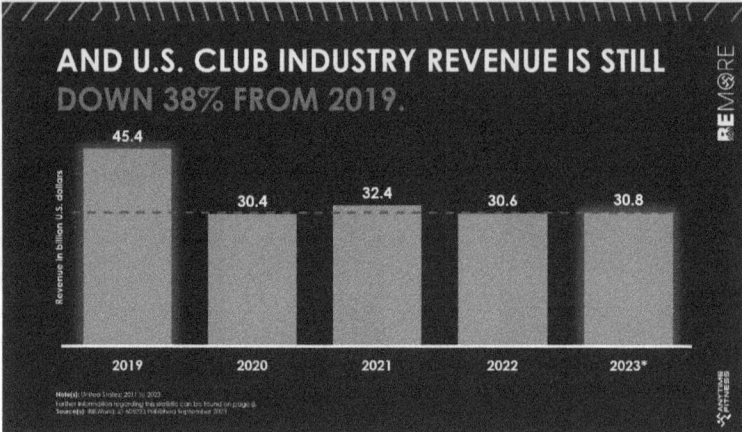

Total gym industry revenue in the U.S.: down.

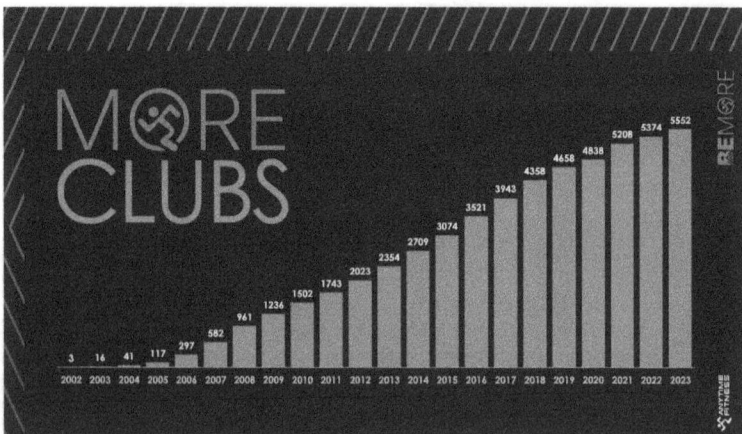

Anytime Fitness: UP!

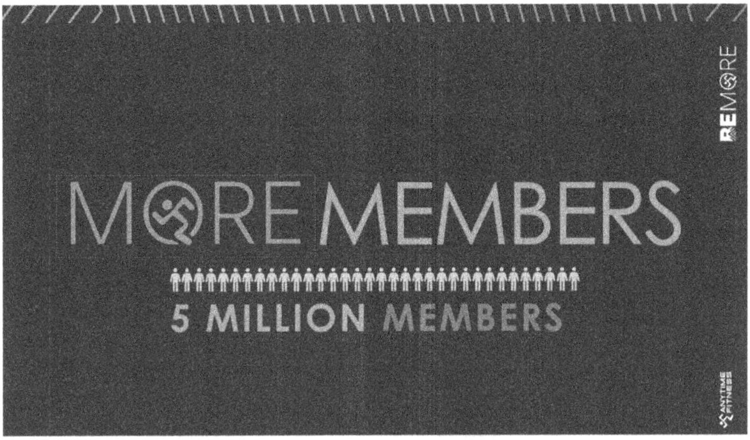

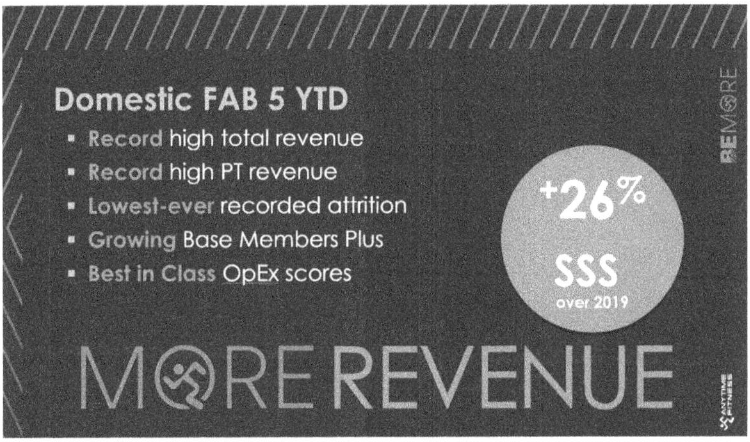

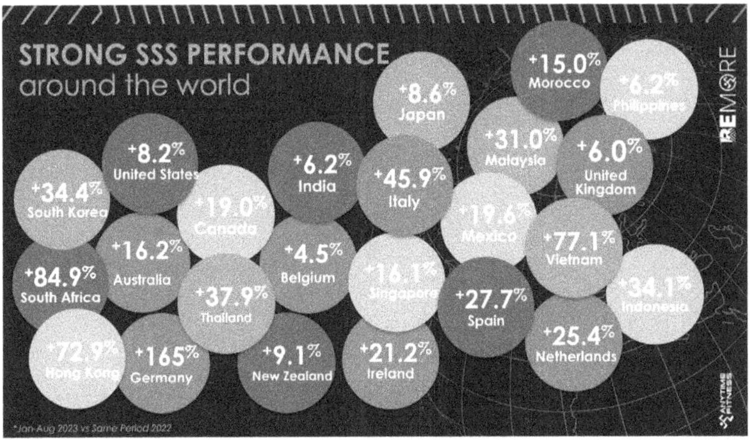

That's the power of a Fanchise!

FANCHISE "QUESTION & ACTION" ITEMS

For Franchisees

Question: If everything stopped tomorrow, how long could you keep the doors open?

> **Action**: Map out a clear reserve plan for fixed costs, payroll and your own salary in a crisis.

Question: Who would you call first if your business was in trouble, and would they take that call?

> **Action**: Ask yourself: *Have I built strong, trust-based relationships with my franchisor, fellow owners and vendors before I need their help?*

Question: If you had to serve your customers without your current location, how would you do it?

> **Action**: Develop a "pivot plan" to keep delivering value when your primary channel is disrupted.

For Franchisors

Question: When crisis hits, will your first message be human or corporate?

> **Action**: Ask yourself: *Am I ready to lead with empathy, transparency and calm before giving operational direction?*

Question: Can you make critical decisions in 24 hours, or does your process slow you down?

> **Action**: Make sure you have a rapid-response team and a decision-making system built for speed and clarity.

Question: Are your support systems built for convenience, or survival?

> **Action**: Ask yourself: *If everything went wrong tomorrow, would our tools, coaching and communication still be lifelines for our owners?*

[12]

FOUND IN TRANSLATION: TAKING YOUR *FANCHISE* GLOBAL

WHEN LIBBY JUNKER, the genius behind our Anytime Fitness conferences, first pitched us on producing an Olympic-style opening ceremony for our franchisee conference in Lake Placid, NY, in 2016, we were skeptical. She envisioned country delegations and flag bearers marching into Herb Brooks Arena, site of the legendary "Miracle on Ice" American victory over the Soviet hockey team in 1980. To us, it sounded complicated, time-consuming and over the top.

We were wrong.

When the day came and we watched franchisees of all ages from dozens of countries march in under their national banners, we couldn't believe what we were seeing and feeling.

Slowly, the arena filled with purple-clad *Fanchisees* carrying flags from Australia, Japan, the United Kingdom, Spain, Chile, India and other countries we never imagined we'd be in when we opened our first club in 2002.

Something profound washed over us. We were standing in the very arena where perhaps the greatest upset in sports history took place, watching our own underdog story expand in real time.

We started as two blue-collar guys from the east side of St. Paul, Minnesota, with high school educations and a crazy idea about 24/7 gyms. No business school training. No venture capital backing. No grand plan for global domination. We were underdogs in every sense of the word, going up against established fitness juggernauts with deeper pockets and decades of experience.

"

Here we were, standing in the very arena where perhaps the greatest upset in sports history took place, watching our own underdog story expand in real time.

"

Yet here we stood, watching people celebrate not just a business they'd bought into, but an *international* brand and Global *Fanchise* they'd fallen in love with. These weren't just franchisees; they were hardcore fans of a mission that transcended borders, languages and cultures.

*Here comes the Australian delegation that flew 20
hours to be here ...*

*Here comes the Japanese delegation wearing pins
collected from previous conferences ...*

*Here come the European delegates who coordinated
matching outfits for their entrance ...*

Enter Canada ... Mexico ... Singapore ... India ...

As each delegation received thunderous applause, we realized that we were witnessing something that goes beyond international business expansion. We were seeing proof that, like music and sports, a true *Fanchise* is universal. The passion, the purpose, the sense of belonging that our small team had created in a corner of the Upper Midwest had found its way into communities around the world.

*A "family photo" of international AF
franchisees at our HQ in Minnesota*

Anytime Fitness had expanded to dozens of countries in one decade — a pace of international growth that would be virtually impossible through corporate development alone. Today, we have more clubs (and bring in more revenue) outside the U.S. than inside it. Nearly 50 official languages are spoken across our locations, and our key fob system might represent the single largest 24/7 access system in the world.

If you belong to an Anytime Fitness club in South Bend, Indiana, then your fob will also open the door of a club in Tokyo. How symbolic is that?

As we watched the "delegations" and remembered the Miracle on Ice, we realized that the true miracle wasn't just that we'd taken our franchise global. It was that it still felt like one big unified family stretched across dozens of nations — one big global *Fanchise*.

Our international con-ferences bear that out. They feel remarkably like our domestic ones, but that's not because we micromanage them. There's no blueprint, no PowerPoint deck that every conference organizer has to operate from. They simply get our culture.

Getting ready to host our Global Summit with master franchisees from around the globe.

A TRUE GLOBAL FOOTPRINT

We've talked about the importance of partnerships, and there's no doubt that the global expansion of Anytime Fitness is fueled by strong partnerships with our master franchisees.

With over 4,000 clubs located outside the United States, most people don't know that Anytime Fitness is the #1 brand in these notable markets. As of this writing, we have roughly:

- 1,500 clubs in Japan thanks to our partners at Fast Fitness Japan (FFJ) led by Akira Okuma

- 700 clubs in Australia thanks to our master franchisee partners Rich Peil and Justin McDonnell

- 75 clubs in New Zealand thanks to our master franchisee partner Richard Ball

- 500 clubs in the region of Southeast Asia thanks to our master franchisee partners Luke Guanlao and Johannes Raadsma

- 400 clubs in Canada thanks to our master franchisee partner Jeff Christison

- 225 in the United Kingdom thanks to our master franchisee partners Rich Peil, Justin McDonnell and Marcello Jimenez

- 200 in India thanks to our master franchisee partner Vikas Jain

- 150 in the Netherlands thanks to our master franchisee partner Petro Hameleers

- 150 in Mexico thanks to our master franchisee partner Rodrigo Chavez

- 100 in Italy thanks to our master franchisee partner Domenic Mercuri

- 75 in Spain, which are corporate owned by Purpose Brands

- (And of course, 1 in Antarctica)

We've planted flags in many existing and emerging markets around the world, including South Africa, Morocco, France, Germany, Ireland, Austria, Qatar, Saudi Arabia, UAE, Cayman Islands, Colombia, South Korea, Vietnam, *and more coming soon.*

CHOOSING THE MODEL

Different models exist for taking a franchise global. We decided that the "master franchisor" model was the best way for us to create an international *Fanchise*. In simple terms, that means we've systematically identif- ied key people across the

Direct vs. Master Franchising Models

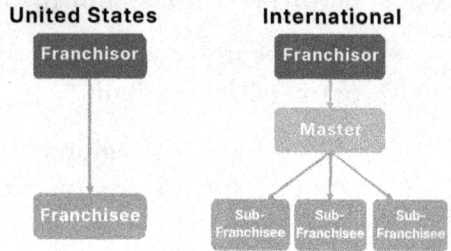

world. Rather than micromanaging them from Minnesota, we've trusted them to understand our brand as well as their culture, and merge the two.

> **What we've really franchised isn't a business; it's a culture.**
>
> — Stacy Anderson

In this model, the "master" manages the language and currency issues, the competitive landscape, the legal and compliance environment, the operational and tech support. Each of these areas can be profoundly complex. For example, some countries today are almost entirely cashless. How will that affect billing? It's not easy to figure that out from 3,000 miles away.

Our alternative was to take a top-down approach, maintain more corporate control, and basically try to 3D-print our product, operations and culture exactly the same in multiple countries.

Franchisors who take this approach might say, "Germany's a big market; let's go there!" They might put a regional agent on the ground in Munich, but they'll still have the corporate office back in the States handle the marketing, technology, operations, coaching of franchisees, etc.

Representing 40+ countries, our international master franchisees come to Minnesota once a year to connect and learn from each other.

The benefit of the "direct" model is that it's centralized and controlled. The risk is that it can be wildly inefficient if, say, a franchisor based in Indianapolis doesn't understand the nuances of running a franchise business in Argentina.

From our perspective, the "master" model is a better way to *Fanchise* a franchise, for four reasons:

1. The "master" who has accountability for the franchisor's success in a particular culture already *knows* that culture.

2. The master knows the nuts and bolts of languages, currencies and marketing in that region.

3. The master can hire local suppliers and other partners in the region, rather than sourcing everything from companies that are thousands of miles away.

4. Like a franchisee in a local market, the master infuses time, money and passion into their own market while leveraging the franchisor's resources to supplement their capabilities.

Put another way, it's a lot harder to build a *Fanchise* when your prospective fans feel like you're not "one of them." The master–franchisee system helps you feel "local" no matter where you are.

MASTERING THE MASTERS

The fundamental difference between domestic and master franchisees lies in their scope and responsibilities. Domestic franchisees focus on executing your proven system at the unit level. Masters must become franchisors themselves — recruiting, training and supporting multiple franchisees while adapting the franchise brand to local cultures, languages, currencies, customs and market conditions without losing its essence.

To a franchisor, finding a "master" to introduce your brand to another country can feel like choosing a co-founder for an entirely new market. Unlike domestic franchisees, who operate individual units within an established system, master franchisees become the face, voice and operational backbone of your brand in their country or region. They're diplomats.

Luke Guanlao and Johannes Raadsma, co-founders and group CEOs at Inspire Brands Asia (parent company of Anytime Fitness Asia), both went from managing individual Anytime Fitness clubs to stepping into a master franchisee role in Southeast Asia. Both describe the transition as involving a heavier burden of fiduciary and emotional responsibility.

"I could stay in my own lane as an individual franchisee, but you can't do that in the master role," says Luke. "As a master, you have to ensure that the entire ecosystem is flourishing and profitable."

Johannes echoes this: "An individual franchisee can be self-interested because you're only looking at your local community," he says. "But as a master franchisor, you have to shift to 'collective interest.' In our current roles, we're probably managing over 400 individual relationships."

Because we're people-focused, the master route always made sense for Anytime Fitness. To be honest, we haven't always gotten it right. Early in our international expansion, we made the mistake of prioritizing financial capability over cultural fit, operational excellence, and fitness and franchise experience.

We signed one particular master who looked great on paper (significant capital, impressive business credentials, ambitious growth projections), but we didn't know whether they truly understood franchising or shared our values around supporting individual franchisees. Long story short: The relationship deteriorated, and we eventually had to take back the territory. It was expensive and time-consuming, and it temporarily damaged our reputation in that market. But it had to be done.

The good news: We licked our wounds, found a new master a few years later, and this is now one of our highest-performing markets. Learning from that one mistake has been priceless.

HOW TO IDENTIFY A MASTER *FANCHISEE*

For franchisors, vetting a potential master *Fanchisee* starts with inviting them to visit you on your home turf, then visiting them on theirs to see how they operate in the culture they should know best. In addition, a franchisor should look for these traits in a master:

- They don't just like your product, service, values and purpose. They *love* them and can translate them into *their* culture.

- They have either franchising or industry experience (finding both can be a challenge). Our Australian master franchisees didn't have prior franchising experience, but they had worked in fitness for decades.

- They have an operator mentality. Each of our master franchisees has been a unit operator in the past, but they also know the difference between operating one of our clubs and being a franchisor.

- They have sufficient capital — not just for territory fees but also for the long-term investment required to build a sustainable system.

We list "capital" last, because it truly shouldn't be your #1 consideration. For example, as we looked at four potential master franchisors for Australia, we ended up choosing the one who was the least financially viable on paper. The difference: They had traveled and visited over 50 of our clubs and they knew our brand almost as well as we did. They've been phenomenally successful.

If you're a franchisor looking to expand internationally, don't get too enamored with deep pockets. We once brought in a master franchisee who was probably the richest guy in his country. But once he signed the deal, his engagement dropped and we had to find a better one. You want a master who's as invested in you as you are in them.

"

If you're a franchisor looking to expand internationally, don't get too enamored with deep pockets.

"

As with all elements of *Fanchising*, finding a master franchisee comes down to culture and value fit — finding partners who are grounded in the purpose side, and who take the *business* seriously but not themselves.

"GLOCALIZATION": BALANCING BRAND CONSISTENCY WITH CULTURAL NUANCE

The unbreakable elements of a proven concept sometimes have to rub up against strong traditions and deeply held cultural norms. For that reason, many franchise brands struggle to "glocalize." That's combining "global" and "local" — asking which franchise standards should be upheld around the world (in every country) and which operational components can be localized for that specific country or region.

One of the biggest mistakes franchisors make when going global is assuming that what works in Kansas will work in Kuwait. The art of adapting your global brand to local markets requires a delicate balance between maintaining your core brand identity and respecting the cultural nuances that can make or break your success.

Take Anytime Fitness's signature 24/7 access model. It's not an exaggeration to say that it revolutionized fitness in the U.S. But in some Middle Eastern countries, round-the-clock access can create challenges around gender dynamics and cultural expectations. Our master franchisees had to thoughtfully implement women-only hours during certain periods, ensuring we maintained our accessibility promise while respecting local customs. Our core value — convenient access to fitness — remained intact, but the execution required cultural sensitivity.

Language presents another glocalization challenge. It's not just about translating your company name into local languages. It's about understanding how fitness concepts, motivation and community-building translate across cultures. What motivates someone to get fit in Japan might be fundamentally different from what drives someone in Colombia, even though the physical act of working out remains the same.

Sometimes your core values need to trump perceived cultural nuances. For example, our Australian Anytime Fitness franchisees began to resist our U.S. tradition of sharing Member Success Stories at their franchisee conferences, calling them "too woo-woo" for their culture. After showing them the emotional impact these stories have at other international conferences, our wonderful Aussies realized they'd made a mistake. They re-adapted the format to feel more authentically Australian while preserving the core purpose of celebrating transformation and community. *Woo-woo for the win-win!*

Some of our European markets have found American sales tactics to be too "aggressive" and/or culturally inappropriate, so they've taken a more consultative, relationship-based app-roach to membership sales. Our master franchisees have adapted their sales training to reflect these preferences while maintaining our

"These Member Success Stories are way too woo-woo."

212

focus on helping people achieve their fitness goals.

Luke and Johannes have masterfully adapted the Anytime Fitness brand to honor Southeast Asian cultural preferences while maintaining our core brand integrity. Their most notable innovation came after they realized that Filipino gym-goers like to train with their friends instead of alone. They wanted to create functional group fitness areas with synthetic purple turf in their clubs in the Philippines.

A top-down international franchise would have balked at the idea, saying it was noncompliant with their brand standards. As a *Fanchise*, we said, *Hey, if that's what the market needs, then let's give it to them.* "Now when you see purple turf in Anytime Fitness gyms all over the world," says Luke, "I dare say that piece of the design was born out of the Philippines through us pushing for the cultural nuance to be respected."

Other Southeast Asia cultural adaptations include party-like grand openings that incorporate local customs, like a traditional lion dance in Singapore; and focusing on Zumba classes, which have such wide popularity in part of Southeast Asia that some of the instructors are considered celebrities.

The franchisors who struggle internationally are those who try to impose American (or home country) solutions on foreign problems. The ones who succeed understand that while your brand promise should remain consistent across the world, your delivery methods have to be flexible enough to honor local cultures while maintaining the integrity of what made your franchise successful in the first place.

DON'T EXPECT OVERNIGHT GLOBAL SUCCESS

Even if a franchisor chooses the more decentralized "master franchisor" route to global expansion, it's critical to know how

213

international units are performing. If one thing still needs to be centralized in your model, it's data.

But it's also important to take a long-term approach and be patient. In our system, we require new masters to own a corporate club for the first year or two so they can get their feet wet and build a model to replicate. In general, we've found that it takes our master franchisees 3–5 years to ramp up their franchise business. During those years, the growth can look slow to nonexistent. Then they reach a tipping point and take off like a rocket.

"

While your brand promise should remain consistent across the world, your delivery methods have to be flexible enough to honor local cultures while maintaining the integrity of what made your franchise successful in the first place. "

India provides a great case in point. For years, we saw steady, moderate growth in that country. We knew we had the right master, but he was working in a place where the very concept of franchising was new. Today, he's reached the tipping point. After 10 years, he opened his 150th club, and he's on track to hit 250 in a fraction of that time.

Remember: a Global Fanchise Isn't the Same as an "International Brand"

Many franchise systems claim to have an "international brand." Often, that simply means that they've taken their domestic product, service and operations, and photocopied them into different countries. Their home country is still the hub of ideas and implementation. Other countries are simply "spokes."

A Global *Fanchise* is something different. With anything you do, you immediately think first about how it will impact the brand globally. It's a complete circulatory system in which ideas and strategies are generated and shared from all around the world for the benefit of the entire system. Innovation has no hub. The biggest idea can come from the smallest country. Communication and the sharing of best practices is a constant and relentless process, and the bar is constantly being raised.

Examples:

- Our Benelux (Belgium, The Netherlands, Luxembourg) clubs created an online sign-up system that we can now use across our other European locations.

- A group of our Southeast Asia clubs have created a highly successful 15-minute onboarding process that can be replicated in thousands of other locations.

- "Recovery" after a workout is proving popular in New Zealand, so we're putting infrared saunas and red-light therapy in our U.S. gyms.

- Our Australian system has helped us strengthen our compliance and brand standards with solid metrics. Their high standards help them boast the best annual unit volumes in our system, which inspires other markets to raise the bar.

Knowledge sharing — especially on a global level — doesn't happen by accident. Every Anytime Fitness international region gets together in person and over Zoom to share best practices regularly.

Another benefit of building a global *Fanchise*: The master system paves the way to open other franchise businesses in the same markets. Once a master franchisee achieves success in their region, they'll likely look for more franchise brands to add. When that happens, the global benefits of the franchise model become ... well, global.

WITNESSING AN INTERNATIONAL *FANCHISE*

STACY ANDERSON SENT this message to her team back home after experiencing an Anytime Fitness conference in Thailand in the summer of 2025.

Team AF,

I wanted to express my deep appreciation for each of you and take a moment to reflect on the impact you're making here and around the world.

While it's easy to assume we are just in the business of franchising gyms, if you look a bit deeper, you realize we are really in the business of *creating freedom for others* — providing opportunities to earn a good living, empowering people to live healthier, more fulfilling lives, and helping people unlock their full potential in ways they never imagined.

217

I recently returned from a conference in Thailand, where 700+ Anytime Fitness owners, staff and partners came together to celebrate our incredible growth in that region.

The Anytime Fitness conference in Thailand, 2025

As the lights dimmed, the opening ceremony started with the flags of each country, carried by a franchisee or staff member up to the stage — each country announced with their teams screaming and cheering. *Singapore! Vietnam!* My eyes started filling up with tears. *Hong Kong! Malaysia!* I looked over at our master franchisees, then at their wives and kids, who beamed with pride as their sacrifices were turned into a movement bigger than any one person. *Indonesia! Taiwan! Philippines!*

There were so many incredible moments at that conference. But beyond the celebration, there was something deeper. In regions of the world where access to opportunity is sometimes limited, where human rights are sometimes challenged,

Suraj Mishra, a multi-unit, multi-country owner operating clubs in Singapore and Malaysia

where safety and security aren't assumed, Anytime Fitness is giving people something life-changing. We're offering the chance for people to make a good, honest living. To provide their families security. To improve the health of their communities so they can build a better future. To truly change the trajectory of their lives.

218

I hope you can feel the magnitude of what you are a part of. In the day-to-day of corporate life, it's easy to get bogged down by the small stuff. But I want you to know what I know deep in my bones: What you do matters — not just in the U.S. but around the world.

- You're the reason someone has a job they love.

- You're the reason someone can feed their family and send their kids to school.

- You're the reason someone feels safe, strong and confident.

Stacy posing with Anytime Fitness Brand Ambassador Fathini Haryanthie

- You're the reason someone can pick up their grandchild.

- You're the reason someone is alive *and thriving*.

- You're the reason for someone's freedom.

Thank you for everything you do. Go celebrate the fact that you are helping create independence around the world by giving people the tools and opportunities to create their own freedom. And take a minute to say, "Wow, just look what we've done!"

With deep gratitude,

— Stacy

FANCHISE "QUESTION & ACTION" ITEMS

For Franchisees

Question: If your brand's reach went global tomorrow, how would you help carry its culture forward?

> **Action**: Name one element of your business today that would make someone on the other side of the world instantly recognize it as part of the same family.

Question: What can you learn from peers operating in completely different cultural contexts?

> **Action**: Ask yourself: *Am I willing to adapt a great idea from halfway around the world even if it challenges the way I've always done things?*

Question: Have you found the balance between brand consistency and local personality?

> **Action**: Ask yourself: *Does my business feel distinctly mine while still unmistakably part of the larger Fanchise?*

For Franchisors

Question: Would your culture survive translation without you in the room?

Action: Write down a brand purpose that's so clear it would be instantly recognized in any language and in any market.

Question: Do you choose international partners for cultural alignment first, financials second?

Action: Ask yourself: *Am I confident my masters care as much about supporting their franchisees as I do?*

Question: Are you flexible enough to adapt without losing your promise?

Action: Determine the areas of your business where you'll consider "global brand standards" versus where you'll need to take a more global approach.

[13]

THE ANNUAL CONFERENCE: BRINGING THE *FANCHISE* TOGETHER

OPENING NIGHT AT our 2015 conference in Lake Placid, NY, was an experience we'll never forget. After the country-by-country procession we talked about in the previous chapter, our plan was to play a Member Success Story video, then have the featured member give a speech. USA "Miracle on Ice" hero Mike Eruzione would give the keynote speech. The cherry on top: The featured member would come back to light a torch and officially begin the conference.

That sequence would have been memorable enough, but something subtle and unexpected happened along the way that stands as one of our top *Fanchise* moments (and led to the photo on the cover of this book).

The Member Success Story video told the story of a young Marine named Matt Pietro. Two weeks before Matt was deployed to Iraq in 2007, he and his wife lost a baby to miscarriage. Soon after arriving in Iraq, he learned that his wife wanted a divorce.

Returning home after a second deployment, Matt fell into a deep depression. He started drinking excessively, gained a ton of weight and felt borderline suicidal. On July 16, 2013, he got into a horrific motorcycle accident that led to his right leg being amputated.

Anytime Fitness member Matt Pietro at our conference in Lake Placid, 2016

Having reached rock bottom, Matt eventually found the courage to wheel himself into an Anytime Fitness club in Hudson Falls, NY. Owner Scott Daley, a fellow veteran, offered to personally train him. In a remarkable show of empathy, Scott taped up his own right leg so he couldn't use it. Matt couldn't believe his eyes as Scott stood on one leg and said, "Get out of the chair, Matt. Let's go."

Our audience of franchisees sat riveted, learning that after two years of training with Scott, Matt lost 170 pounds, competed in multiple Spartan races and changed his entire outlook on life. After showing Matt doing one-legged burpees (try that sometime), the video ended with him saying, "It's not the physicality of the person that determines whether or not they're going to be successful in reaching their goals. It's all heart, will and passion."

The crowd went berserk.

Matt came up in his wheelchair and spoke, and the crowd dabbed their eyes as they stood and applauded.

Now it was Mike Eruzione's turn. Mike scored the game-winning goal against the Soviet hockey team in the very arena where we now sat. Ever since, he's arguably been *the* American symbol of the hardworking underdog triumphing over adversity through sheer force of will.

After Mike told the riveting story of that magical night on Febrary 22, 1980, we presented him with a replica Anytime Fitness–branded USA Olympic hockey sweater with his name printed on the back. He put it on to applause from the crowd of 2,500+. And then the most amazing thing happened.

As Mike left the stage, he walked toward Matt Pietro at the edge of the ice. Privately, while the audience was still clapping, he told Matt what a hero he thought he was, and how much he looked up to him for beating his own odds and turning his

Mike Eruzione removes his jersey to give it to Matt Pietro.

life around. He choked up as he put his hand on Matt's shoulder and said, "You're an inspiration to me." Then he took off his jersey and handed it to him.

Keep in mind, Mike could have said all of this in front of the audience and made himself look even better than he already had. But he didn't. He chose to say it privately, without a microphone, because it truly was about Matt, not him.

> **While the audience was still clapping, [Mike Eruzione] told Matt what a hero he thought he was, and how much he looked up to him for beating his own odds and turning his life around. Then he took off his jersey and handed it to him.**

We concluded the opening ceremonies by inviting Matt back up to the stage to light the torch, and he did it while wearing Eruzione's jersey.

We had just witnessed the guy known for one of the greatest sports achievements in history telling one of our members that *he's* the real hero. By extension, we knew that Scott Daley, Matt's trainer and just one of our many amazing franchisees around the world, was *also* a hero.

Again, the hard work and passion of our entire team — over the course of 14 years — led to one magical *Fanchise* moment that we'll never forget.

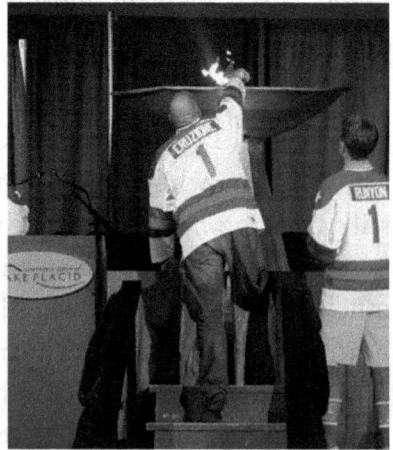

Pietro lights the torch to officially start our Lake Placid conference.

6 STRATEGIES TO *FANCHISE* A CONFERENCE

Some franchise systems see an annual conference[21] as an obligation. We see it as an opportunity — the precious moment when your entire system comes together to learn, laugh, cry, connect, party, reflect, celebrate and hopefully go back to their global hometowns inspired to transform their businesses and their lives.

Whether you're a single-unit franchisee or an emerging franchisor, becoming a *Fanchise* means seeing your system's conference as an opportunity. There's no cookie-cutter way to do it, but in this chapter, we're going to share some of the techniques that have turned Anytime Fitness conferences around the world into events that feel more like religious revivals.

From a franchisor perspective, it helps when you have an absolute rock star in charge of organizing and executing the event. For us, that's been the previously mentioned Libby Junker, who has designed and produced every conference we've had since we rented a modest riverboat in St. Paul for our very first one.

The Anytime Fitness Japanese delegation arrives to opening night at one of our conferences.

We asked Libby to narrow her advice down to a few key strategies. We list them below, and we're going to start with one of our own:

---

[21] Ours started annually, then moved to every other year.

227

Strategy #1: Make Leadership Accessible and Approachable

We can't tell you how many times a supplier, partner or franchisee has approached one of us at an Anytime Fitness conference and said, "I can't believe you're hanging out with us." We're surprised that other franchise founders and leaders *don't* hang out with their partners. Some even restrict themselves to VIP sections and basically swoop in and out.

To our fellow franchisor leaders, here's some tough love: You're not a rock star. You're a business leader in a field that's all about people. You should make yourself accessible to all of your franchisees, even if they're a mom-and-pop with only one unit. It shows how much you value them, and we've even converted some previously disgruntled franchisees into true believers just by taking the time to talk to them at our conference.

> **To our fellow franchisor leaders, here's some tough love: You're not a rock star. You're a business leader in a field that's all about people. You should make yourself accessible to all of your franchisees, even if they're a mom-and-pop with only one unit.**

Strategy #2: Start the Planning with Clear Purpose and Transformation Goals

Every great conference begins long before the first speaker takes the stage. As Libby puts it, "I start every conference by asking everyone on my team one question: 'When this conference is over, how do we want people to *think* differently, and what do we want them to *do* differently?'"

Even before you choose a theme, you need to know exactly what mindset shift you're trying to create, because it's about *transformation.*

Frankly, most franchise conferences fail because they focus on the wrong metrics. They measure success by attendance numbers, speaker ratings or how smoothly everything ran. All of that is important, but the real question is whether your franchisees leave thinking and acting differently than when they arrived. Are they more committed to the brand? Do they have new strategies for their businesses? Have they connected with other franchisees who can help them succeed?

If you can't answer these questions with specificity, then you're just throwing a really expensive party.

The business-oriented answers to this question usually come first. *We want improved operations, new revenue streams and better marketing strategies!* But we've learned that the emotional connection is what matters. When a conference inspires everyone to reconnect with the reason they fell in love with the franchise in the first place, then it's a success.

This approach requires discipline. It's tempting to add every good idea or speaker opportunity to the mix and see what sticks. But if it doesn't serve your emotional goals, then it doesn't belong at your conference. Every session, activity and social event must support the emotional transformation.

Strategy #3: Design for All Five Senses and Create Emotional Connection

Human beings don't just process information through PowerPoint slides and breakout sessions. We're sensory creatures who form memories through sight, sound, taste, smell and touch.

Going back to fandom in music and sports, we all know that going to a game or concert is a multisensory experience.

A conference attendee getting ready to go down the Lake Placid Olympic ski jump hill at 50 mph

As Chuck talked about earlier in this book, he's been fortunate to experience a concert at the Sphere in Las Vegas. It's no accident that the Sphere not only features pristine sound and visuals but also includes haptic seats that help people "feel" sound vibrations, as well as machines that create wind, temperature and even scent effects.

Appealing to the senses is a Libby specialty. "I try to hit all of them at every conference," she says. "I want everyone who's there to see, hear, feel, smell and taste something different. It started when we had a conference in Wisconsin. I built bonfires outside so everyone arriving could take in that North Woods smell, and the strategy stuck."

CHUCK & DAVE'S TOP 5 CONFERENCE *FANCHISE* MOMENTS

Chuck

Our First Member Success Stories in 2005

I'll never forget standing next to our OG members as they shared how our brand had changed their lives. Our conferences are a lot slicker today, but the best part is still when a member accepts their award and speaks from the heart.

The Night the "MFCEO" Was Born

We rented out the Crazy Horse Saloon in Nashville and hired the band Lo-Cash. When the band called me and Dave to the

stage and asked me what I did, I looked out into the audience and yelled, "I'm the motherf***ing CEO!" The moniker "MFCEO" stuck. More importantly, seeing me let loose gave our fans permission to have as much fun as possible.

"Saveheart" Video

As we've mentioned earlier in this book, showing this video in 2009 created a *Fanchise* rallying cry and brought us closer together as a tribe. It also kicked off a tradition of opening-night conference videos that infused a healthy dose of Play into our culture.

"Thank-You Notes"

We made a video of me doing a version of Jimmy Fallon's Tonight Show "Thank-You Notes" routine and showed it at our conference in Scottsdale, AZ. It was so popular that doing a live version became the way we end every conference.

Lake Placid International Opening Ceremony

To be in the arena where the *Miracle on Ice* actually happened and see our international franchisees march in one by one under their country's flags really drove home the global *Fanchise* we were now a part of.

Dave

A "Holy S***" Moment

Chuck and I shared a cocktail before going on stage one year at an opening night and had a heartfelt moment of realizing what we've done together.

The Confetti Celebration

After our Saturday-night awards ceremony in Nashville, we littered the conference hall with confetti to celebrate a major milestone on our *Fanchise* journey. The place erupted, and the fact that my mom and dad were there made it extra special.

Member and Franchisee Success Stories

At every conference, we spend the last night handing out awards to our members and franchisees, and listening to their heartfelt speeches. I can't pinpoint any particular conference or story. They're all amazing, and they get to me every time.

Meeting My Future Wife

This one's personal: I met my wife for the first time at our 2021 conference in Dallas, TX. I was an instant fan.

Sharing the Experience with My Kids

My kids have practically grown up at Anytime Fitness conferences over the years. It's been amazing to see them embrace the brand, the people, the stories and the entire experience.

When you think about your life's most memorable experiences, they weren't just intellectual; they engaged your entire being. The smell of your grandmother's kitchen, the sound of your favorite song at a pivotal moment, the first bite of a dish that became your favorite food. When you design a conference experience that touches all the senses, you pave the way for those same kinds of powerful, lasting memories.

A behind-the-scenes shot from our Hangover conference parody video

Keep in mind that different people respond to different sensory triggers, which is why you need variety in your approach. Some franchisees will be more moved by the visual spectacle of your opening ceremony. Others will connect more deeply with intimate conversations during a fireside chat. Still others will find their breakthrough moment in hands-on workshops where they can touch and manipulate new tools or products.

"

When you think about your life's most memorable experiences, they weren't just intellectual; they engaged your entire being.

"

When you design for all five senses, you ensure that every attendee has multiple opportunities to form meaningful connections with your brand and community.

Strategy #4: Ultimately, It's All About People & Networking

Here's a truth that most franchise systems miss: The formal education sessions at conferences aren't where the real learning happens. Anyone can get training videos, operational updates and best practices through webinars, documentation and other tools. What they can't get anywhere else is the opportunity to connect with peers who understand their exact challenges. As Libby discovered, "The real value for franchisees at our conference is meeting those people at lunch who are facing the same issues they're facing. That's what they leave with."

If you're a franchisor, this insight completely changes how you structure your conference. It took us a few years to figure it out. In fact, it was our European franchisees who really pushed the idea: *Instead of cramming every minute of the conference with content, space it out a little,* they told us. *Build in networking time. Let the lunch break go two or three hours instead of one. Extend the cocktail receptions. Create peer-to-peer sessions where franchisees can share war stories and solutions.*

This might feel counterintuitive. Everyone invests time and money in the conference, so the natural impulse is to pack as much content into it as possible to prove its value. But we've heard it from our franchisees and suppliers for years: The connections

AF conference attendees do a massive workout in Nashville led by a Member Success Story winner who became a personal trainer.

they make during nonstructured periods at our conferences are even more valuable than what's delivered from the main stage.

Effective networking creates a virtuous *Fanchise* cycle. People who form strong peer relationships at a conference become more engaged with the brand overall, making them more likely to implement new initiatives, give constructive feedback and commit to long-term success. They also become active ambassadors who encourage other franchisees to attend future conferences — making each event a highly anticipated reunion, as well as an educational opportunity.

"

Effective networking creates a virtuous *Fanchise* cycle. People who form strong peer relationships at a conference become more engaged with the brand overall, making them more likely to implement new initiatives, give constructive feedback and commit to long-term success.

"

Strategy #5: Make Everyone Feel Like an Owner

When people feel like they own something — a business, a project or an experience — they invest more energy, take more pride and show more commitment. Libby discovered this as we grew and started moving our conference locations all over the United States (today, our master franchisees run conferences all over the world).

"For many of our franchisees, our conference is their vacation, their chance for team building," Libby says. "They get so excited when we choose a location that's close to them. They end up co-hosting the event and offering to help, because they feel a sense of ownership around it."

The ownership principle also applies to vendor/supplier relationships. Too many conferences treat suppliers as second-class citizens — necessary for funding but not integral to the experience. Smart conference organizers flip this dynamic on its head by making vendors feel like true partners in the franchise system's success.

We've long made a point of treating our suppliers as true partners in our franchise ecosystem and at our conferences. "We tell franchisees, 'Hey, you couldn't exist without these guys!'" says Libby. "Some of our suppliers bring more people to our conference than to any other one they attend. They love the experience, but they also get more business, so they can justify it."

One specific tactic we use for suppliers is our "Passport Program." To win a prize at the end of the conference, our franchisees have to visit every supplier booth and get a stamp for each. (When it comes to the prize, we don't mess around. As you'll see, we've even given away cars.) Suppliers also receive the same branded lanyards as franchisees. They're invited to all the same social events and networking functions. And we make a point of taking some of them out to dinner and footing the bill, instead of the other way around.

The result: Our suppliers bring more energy and creativity to our partnership because they feel like integral members of our family rather than companies trying to sell something. Some of them even have Anytime Fitness tattoos to prove it.

Strategy #6: Target the Front-Runners to Convert the Middle

Every franchisor basically has three groups of franchisees: the passionate advocates, the coasters and the resisters. Most conference organizers make the mistake of trying to design content that appeals to everyone, which usually results in generic programming that doesn't appeal to anyone.

AF conference attendees enjoying an outdoor concert in Louisville, KY

As Libby learned through experience, "I gear the conference for the front-runner group because they're going to convince and convert the middle group better than I can."

This strategy means resisting the temptation to focus on your most vocal critics. The franchisees who complain the loudest often get the most attention, but they're rarely the best representatives of the broader system. Meanwhile, your biggest advocates — the ones who are already implementing best practices, driving innovation and achieving strong results — sometimes get taken for granted. When you design your conference to celebrate and amplify these front-runners, you create a positive and contagious energy.

❝

The franchisees who complain the loudest often get the most attention, but they're rarely the best representatives of the broader system. **❞**

Does this mean franchisors should ignore the middle group or write off the resisters entirely? No. They should create an environment where positive peer pressure works in their favor. When the most successful franchisees get excited about new initiatives, talk enthusiastically about the brand and share their results openly, coasters have a harder time staying unmotivated. When they see concrete evidence of what's possible, even some of the resisters will come around. If they don't, then they weren't going to be converted by your conference anyway.

BONUS INSIGHT: CREATE CONSEQUENCES FOR NONATTENDANCE

Influencing people's behavior in a franchise system (or any large system) requires carrots and sticks. Some professions have continuing education credits. We have continuing engagement credits (CECs).

This system requires our Anytime Fitness franchisees to earn 1,200 CECs annually through activities like attending conferences, participating in training sessions, completing online courses or engaging in brand-building activities. We mention them here because attending the conference delivers enough credits for the entire year, and franchisees who don't earn their required credits are fined $1 for every missing one, with the proceeds going to our ad fund.

Despite this "stick," our foundation still annually collects over $200,000 from franchisees who choose to pay the fine rather than engage — though, as Libby notes, "many of those who reluctantly attend conferences to avoid the fine write to us afterwards to tell us that it was a life-changing experience."

A *FANCHISE*
MOMENT FROM OUR
2021 CONFERENCE

STILL EMERGING FROM the Covid-19 pandemic, we held our conference in downtown Dallas in the fall of 2021. Given what we'd all just been through (and were still going through), we knew that this one had to be extra special. So we came up with an idea.

We bought a brand-new $40,000 Jeep, wrapped it in the Anytime Fitness brand, and decided to give it away on the last night of the conference as a prize using the Passport Program we described earlier. Visit all of our suppliers, and you could win a free car. Not bad.

Day after day at the conference, the Jeep nearly stole the show. Sitting at the end of the exhibition hall, it acted like a magnet — drawing gawkers, admirers and wannabe owners for days. More people than ever filled up their Passports for the chance to own that shiny purple Jeep. Everyone wanted it.

The excitement built throughout the last night of the conference. Then, after all the Member Success

Stories had been told, awards handed out and speeches given, Libby Junker and Stacy Anderson took the stage to announce the big winner. A hush fell over the crowd of 2,500+ in the giant ballroom as they drew a name at random.

"Eric _____ from New Jersey, you're the winner!"

The crowd clapped, but the response was notably muted. Everyone was happy for Eric, but they were also jealous. Then a funny thing happened. Nobody ran up to the stage. Eric was nowhere to be found.

"Eric? Eric?"

A murmur pulsed through the crowd. Libby and Stacy allowed for a possible return from a bathroom break. Nothing.

"We're drawing again!" Libby said, and the crowd went crazy.

"Anthony _____ from Washington!" came the next name.

This time, Anthony was there. He ran up to get the keys to his new Jeep. He thanked Eric for not being there (nice touch), and then he did something extraordinary, which no one saw coming.

"I appreciate winning this Jeep, but I know someone who needs it more than I do," he said. "I want to give it to my club manager because she truly deserves it."

The manager came to the stage, and Anthony handed her the keys. She wiped away her tears, and so did at least half the crowd.

We shipped the Jeep to Washington, and the manager gave it a name. She called it "Eric."

Thanks for not showing up, Eric!

243

FANCHISE MOMENT: "BE LEGENDARY"

THE FOLLOWING IS an edited version of an All Staff message we sent in August 2018 — a great example of how your conference can inspire people far beyond their businesses:

The annual conference is an opportunity to rejuvenate 2,500+ people and empower them to climb higher, and we've been intentional about weaving in diverse speakers, new themes and locations, and a playful sense of joie de vivre to take someone's existing mindset and shake it like a snow globe.

If we do it right, we don't just get them to run a high-performance business, we inspire them toward a high-performance life. Last year's conference theme was "Be Legendary," and the message below is from

Ed Hunt, a longtime Anytime Fitness owner who wanted to share a story about his wife:

Be Legendary

If you're not familiar with the action sport of Red Bull Crashed Ice or ice cross downhill, now is the time to look it up. In March 2017, as a longtime fan of the event, I took our family (including my amazing wife, Tara) to see the season finale in Ottawa, Canada. While I didn't know it then, in Tara's mind she was turning over the thought that "I could do that." Tara started spending more time on skates that summer and testing her limits.

In September 2017, the Anytime Fitness conference in Palm Springs was themed "Be Legendary," the takeaway being that you only get one shot at this life, and you might as well make yours the stuff of legends. At some point that week, it all clicked for Tara. She was going to surround herself with champions, train, compete and qualify for Red Bull Crashed Ice.

Fast-forward to a cold January weekend in St. Paul, Minnesota, where, after traveling to Austria to earn points in the B-League known as the Riders Cup, Tara was dropping in on her last qualifying run on the Crashed Ice course. The initial drop was at least 25 feet of vertical ice, and she hadn't landed it yet.

With her hockey shorts stuffed with towels borrowed from the hotel for extra padding, she dropped in and stuck the landing! The acceleration that gravity provides on the near-zero resistance of ice can only really be understood once you experience it, but in short, this initial drop sent Tara rocketing down the ice track packed with jumps, drop-offs and ramps. It was over in less than 50 seconds, but that was all she needed.

In those 50 seconds, Tara became the oldest woman (39 years) to qualify for a Red Bull Crashed Ice event. Over the course of the 2017–18 season, she raced in Austria, America, Finland and Canada, solidifying her legendary status — not just in her community, but in the Red Bull community of elite action-sports athletes.

If Tara were telling you this story, she would tell you that it doesn't have to be downhill ice racing; it just has to be important enough to you to get you so far outside of your comfort zone that you move into legendary territory.

— Ed Hunt

August 2018

FANCHISE "QUESTION & ACTION" ITEMS

For Franchisees

Question: When was the last time you left an event not just informed, but *transformed*?

> **Action:** Approach your next conference with the intent to take one idea, relationship or inspiration home that will change your business and life.

Question: Are you making the most of the networking that happens between the sessions?

> **Action:** The next time you're at a conference, determine who in the room might have the exact solution, encouragement or insight you've been missing, then actively seek them out.

Question: What will you give, not just get, at your next conference?

> **Action:** Figure out a way to offer mentorship, share a hard-won lesson or cheer someone on who might be struggling.

For Franchisors

Question: Do your conferences just fill an agenda, or do they connect the head and the heart?

Action: Design moments that create an emotional shift and reconnect people to why they fell in love with your brand in the first place.

Question: How accessible are you to every franchisee in the room?

Action: Write down five ways you're ensuring that even your smallest or newest owners feel seen, heard and valued.

Question: Are you creating an experience that people can *feel*?

Action: Map out exactly how you're engaging all five senses so your event becomes a lasting memory.

PART III:

FINAL

FANCHISE

THOUGHTS

[14]

RAISE YOUR HAND

Chuck here, and this chapter is a story from my personal life because I couldn't think of a better way to deliver the message. Here goes ...

MY DAUGHTER ELLA plays high school soccer. Her school traditionally has a strong program, and they recently spent the season ranked #1 in the state for schools their size.

In the fall of 2019, they competed in the sectional finals against their biggest and bitterest rival. It was the fourth year in a row that these two teams had met. What was on the line? For these girls, everything. The winner earned not only bragging rights but also the chance to move on to the state tournament, where they would get to play in front of thousands of people inside the Minnesota Vikings' home arena, U.S. Bank Stadium.

On a crisp fall evening under the lights, with students and parents filling the stands, the energy was tense and electric. Like an evenly matched tug-of-war, momentum swung through the game. The refs handed out four yellow cards, which is typically what you see in an MLS or English Premier League match.

At the end of regulation, the score was 2–2. During the regular season, the game would have been over at this point, and both teams would have gotten credit for a tie. But this was the playoffs, so the game went to overtime. After two overtimes, the score remained 2–2, so it was on to a shoot-out.

If you're not familiar with a soccer shoot-out, it presents the ultimate drama and pressure for the players who participate. Five players from each team line up to alternate taking penalty kicks 12 yards away from the goal. Whoever gets the most shots past the goalkeeper wins.

I'd never seen a shoot-out because it only happens in the playoffs, so I didn't know which five players would be chosen from Ella's team. I assumed that they probably practice these kicks, so the coaches already knew which players would have the best chance for success.

When I saw the five players from Ella's team come out, my heart skipped a beat. There she was.

The shoot-out started, and everyone held their breath. The other team shot first and made it. Our team missed, and the other team scored again. We were down 0–2.

Now it was Ella's turn. She stepped into the spotlight, concentrated, stepped back, took her shot and … YES! It shot past the keeper, making it 1–2.

This would be a better story if Ella's team wound up winning the shoot-out and the game, but they didn't. Before long, their rivals were celebrating while our girls were hugging and crying.

But *winning* isn't the point of this story. Ella is going to play hundreds of soccer and basketball games in her life, and while this loss will sting more than most, she and her teammates will recover, rally and continue riding the emotional roller coaster of competitive sports while they acquire valuable life skills.

The real point of the story is what I learned afterward.

As we walked to the car, I had a consoling arm around Ella. I turned to her and said, "So how did you get chosen for the shoot-out?" She was only a sophomore at the time, and I knew that a coach might be more inclined to go with juniors and seniors, especially since the latter might be playing the last game of their high school careers.

Ella shrugged. "The coach asked us who wanted to go out and take the shots, and I raised my hand."

Now I felt like hugging her and crying. My daughter had raised her hand. She had embraced an incredibly stressful moment for an athlete, especially a teenage girl, when many of her older teammates were afraid of the moment. She had also missed penalty kicks during previous seasons of club soccer — so she carried those negative memories with her — and yet she still raised her hand.

As a parent, you do and don't want your daughter in that situation. If she makes the shot, she's a hero. If she misses it, she's the scapegoat. But I was deeply moved knowing that even though Ella is going to make and miss plenty of metaphorical shots throughout her life, she's going to raise her hand.

And that's the point of this story.

There are two types of people in the world: Those who raise their hands and those who don't. I'm not passing judgment on people who don't. Everyone has a logical reason for doing (or not doing) things. But Anytime Fitness built a *Fanchise* by creating a culture of hand-raising at every level of our business — embracing people who show courage and confidence even when

Are you okay, Dad?   *It's dusty in here.*

they have inner doubts and can't control the outcome.

As a franchisor, franchisee, staff member, supplier or investor, you need to raise your hand.

Raise your hand to solve a problem.

Raise your hand to be a leader and get more engaged.

Raise your hand to help a co-worker.

Raise your hand to _____ (you fill in the blank).

And if you want to transform from a franchise into a *Fanchise*, it's not enough to raise your own hand. You need to build a team of hand-raisers. Your employees. Your partners. Every single stakeholder in your business needs to be a hand-raiser.

Ready to build a *Fanchise*? Raise your hand.

[15]

TELL YOUR STORIES

AT OUR VERY first annual conference in St. Paul in 2005, Chuck threw out an idea that felt radical at the time: "Hey, why don't we share some success stories from members of our gyms?"

Not everyone was on board. Remember, back then it was all about our business model: affordable, stripped-down gyms open 24/7. Everyone, including us, was focused on growth. It was about opening as many Anytime Fitness gyms as possible. It was about taking such a commanding lead in this new fitness club category that no one would be able to catch us.

Shouldn't we be 100% focused on new locations and better equipment, marketing, retention and access systems? Who cares about a bunch of touchy-feely "stories"?

Chuck insisted, so we contacted our clubs in a few smaller Minnesota towns like Elk River, Hibbing and Virginia. Our franchisees found members who said they had stories to tell, and we invited them to speak.

Fast-forward to the conference, and these members (including Pat Welsh, who we mentioned previously) took the small stage to a smattering of applause from the relatively small crowd. One by one, they pulled out pieces of crinkled paper with a few handwritten notes scrawled on them and started reading. We had no idea what they were going to say.

At first, it felt awkward. It's funny to think about how primitive these conferences were compared to the ones we're producing today. No one had experience speaking in front of groups. This wasn't a huge hotel ballroom packed with 3,000 people and filled with high-definition video screens. This was as humble as it gets. And yet the emotional impact was there from the start.

As these Anytime Fitness members talked about how our ultra-accessible gyms had helped them lose weight, improve their mental health and change their lives, they got emotional. A catch in the throat. A tear that needed to be wiped. A sniffle. A pause to gather themselves before continuing.

Pretty soon, we were all caught up in the moment — all fighting our emotions, and losing.

That moment changed our business, our franchise and our lives. We needed a reminder that everything we were doing was about transforming lives. Looking back, this (not our business model or anything related to the nuts and bolts of our operations) was the secret ingredient that would evolve us into a *Fanchise*.

> **Pretty soon, we were all caught up in the moment — all fighting our emotions, and losing.**

Imagine learning this in a business program: "The secret to starting and maintaining a successful global franchise is stories, not systems." It'll never happen, but it's true.

Especially in the fitness world, you'd be shocked at how many businesses don't tell stories. In Chapter 12, we talked about how we had to convince our franchisees in Australia to start telling them again after they had lapsed. After the franchisee conference Down Under, Chuck basically had to pull our Aussie leadership team aside and say,

Honoring AF Member Success Story winner Mary Thoma in 2015

"Guys, you just spent three days with all of your franchisees, and you didn't share a single Member Success Story!"

"But Chuck," they said. "Those stories are too soft and 'American' for the culture down here."

Chuck gave them one of his patented looks — which, if you're not familiar, basically says, "You're going to do what I want you to do, and if you don't, you might be an idiot." The Aussies went back to sharing Member Success Stories, and it's made a huge difference.

These days, our franchise owners actually compete to have their members' stories shared. For our U.S. conference, we choose the top three stories and make each into a mini-documentary video worthy of an Oscar. This past year, we received eight member success stories submissions *even before the registration site was live.*

And that's not the only storytelling involved. Our entire brand is about storytelling. We share the successes not only of our members but also of our franchisees. We tell the stories of the most successful franchise systems, the clubs that have done the best job turning themselves around, and the ones that do the most for their local communities.

If you want to become a *Fanchise*, you have to become a storyteller, period.

- Document the most powerful examples of how your business has transformed lives.

- Tell these stories at both the franchisor and individual franchise unit level.

- Create platforms to showcase these stories, whether that's through internal communication, conferences or other events.

- Feature these stories in your marketing materials and training programs. (By the way, they also do wonders for recruitment.)

- Make celebrating successes a regular part of your culture.

Oh, and if these kinds of success stories don't exist, then you have a bigger problem.

[16]

ALWAYS EMBRACE THE 4 Ps

THIS BOOK WOULDN'T be complete without an encore mention of the 4 Ps, so we'll end with one more pitch for you to embrace the unbeatable combination of People, Purpose, Profits and Play.

If you want to create an elite and highly valuable *Fanchise*, then you have to embrace long-term versus short-term thinking in each of these areas.

PEOPLE

You have to invest in your **People** — not just to hit quarterly productivity targets, but for the long term and beyond just their job skills.

PURPOSE

You have to define, communicate and personally demonstrate a meaningful **Purpose** that connects to long-term emotional outcomes, not just short-term financial ones.

PROFITS

Without **Profits**, nothing else is possible. But you have to balance short-term profitability with long-term growth investments.

PLAY

Work has to be fun. You have to embrace authentic elements of **Play** that create genuine bonds among all of your stakeholders.

We'll always see the 4 Ps as the foundation of success. In addition to all the other benefits they bring, we believe that they can unlock the door to becoming a *Fanchise*.

That's our show. We hope you enjoyed it. Now get out there and build your own raving fan base!

Your Biggest Fans,

Chuck & Dave

ACKNOWLEDGMENTS

To Robert Herjavec —

Thank you for writing the foreword to this book. For providing your time, motivation and empathy to our owners during the Covid podcast. And for teaching and inspiring countless people through *Shark Tank*. Congratulations on your fitness transformation, which will hopefully inspire others to follow in your footsteps.

To Marc Conklin —

Thank you for all the creative, silly and playful ideas you've infused into our brands over the years, and for being such a fun, collaborative and superb writing, cigar-smoking and Irish whiskey–drinking partner.

To Our Expert Panel & Editorial Reviewers —

Stacy Anderson, thank you for your wickedly big brain and heart. From CMO to global leader, you've positively impacted the lives of millions.

Joe Fittante, thank you for embodying both purpose and pragmatism in your leadership. We appreciate the help during our most difficult times.

Chuck Modell, thank you for shaping our thinking and our policies to balance Fanchising and Franchising. We're forever grateful.

Ron Gardner, thank you and massive respect for your fairness and seeing all sides of the issues in franchising, and for forcing this industry to be better.

Jim Goniea, thank you for making our company better, safer and more prepared for the future. When you speak, people listen.

Scott Greenberg, thank you for making the franchise industry better one franchisee and franchisor at a time through books, speaking and sharing your valuable experience.

Matt Haller, thank you for your passion to protect and promote the economic and life-changing franchise industry.

Libby Junker, bravo for 20 years of high-performance work, and creating some of the greatest weekends of our lives at our conferences.

Brian Schnell, thank you for your infectious passion and leadership within the franchise industry. You make this industry better!

Susan Walker, thank you for sharing your outsider's perspective to make this book better. You have a gift!

Jess Schneider, thank you for your edits, as well as for saving those dozens of "all staff" emails over the years. They were incredibly useful, and it meant a lot.

Debra Zieman, thank you for your passionate feedback and polish, and for always providing the points of view from our various stakeholders.

Leesa Lund, thank you for supporting both of us over so many years, and for being the best executive assistant and human being on the planet.

Anne Kelley Conklin, thank you for finding and eliminating our mistakes, and making us look way more polished than we are.

Rodney Miles, thank you for your guidance (and cover design chops) in helping us package this book and get it in the hands of our Anytime Fitness family at our most important event.

To the thousands of franchise owners around the world, kudos on investing in yourself and living a purpose-driven life. We have so much work to do and so many more lives to change!

To the thousands of employees who have been a part of this *Fanchise* journey, keep climbing and working with People, Purpose, Profits and Play. We enjoyed every step of the climb together!

And finally, to all our loved ones —
We truly are your biggest fans!

ABOUT THE AUTHORS

Chuck Runyon & Dave Mortensen are two guys from Minnesota who, without a college degree between them, co-founded and grew the world's largest fitness franchise, built a $3.7 billion global wellness empire and created a team, culture and movement that continues to change the lives of millions of people around the world.

www.ingramcontent.com/pod-product-compliance
Lightning Source LLC
Chambersburg PA
CBHW071549210326
41597CB00019B/3169